FAILURE IS NOT THE PROBLEM®:
IT'S THE BEGINNING OF YOUR SUCCESS

FAILURE IS NOT THE PROBLEM®
IT'S THE BEGINNING OF YOUR SUCCESS

George A. Milton
Colonel, U.S. Army Retired

FAILURE IS NOT THE PROBLEM®
It's the Beginning of Your Success
Publisher: Marissa F. Cohen
Publication Date: 2020
Copyright © 2020 by George A. Milton - All Rights Reserved
Printed in USA by Marissa F. Cohen
ISBN 9798617682412
Edited By: Nicole Vitale & LtCol. Ned Cummings, USAF Ret.
Cover Design by: Angie Alaya / Pro_ebookcovers

All rights reserved. No part of this book may be reproduced or transmitted in any form or by any means including, but not limited to electronic, mechanical or information storage and retrieval systems - except in the case of brief quotations embodied in critical reviews and articles - without written permission from the author.

Table of Contents

Dedication	6
Acknowledgments	12
Foreword	15
Preface	17
Introduction	23
Chapter 1 Fear of Failure	26
Chapter 2 Self-Regulation	32
Chapter 3 Failure In a Magical Place	36
Chapter 4 Being Unfit Doesn't Mean Unqualified	39
Chapter 5 Poverty Doesn't Mean Failure	43
Chapter 6 Failure Is About Self-Reflection	49
Chapter 7 Fear of Failure Might Get You on TV	53
Chapter 8 Change Your Mindset Be Disciplined	57
Chapter 9 Famous People Also Fail	61
Chapter 10 Your Attitude Towards Failure Is Important	73
Chapter 11 Failure Unacceptable - Only Win	76
Chapter 12 Failure Is The Big Elephant	80
Chapter 13 Failure Is About Retraining	83
Chapter 14 Failure Can Cause A Lieutenant To Despair	88
Chapter 15 There Is Value In Your Failure	93

Chapter 16 When Failure Makes You Fee Inadequate And People Call YoU Stupid, Never Give Up, Even When You Fail Repeatedly	96
Chapter 17 Failure And Success Are Two Sides Of The Same Coin	99
Chapter 18 When You Fail, Embrace It	102
Chapter 19 My Failure To Become A Chaplain	105
Chapter 20 From Ordinary To Extraordinary	110
Chapter 21 The Chaplain Assistant's Failure	112
Chapter 22 Do Not Punish Yourself When You Fail	117
Chapter 23 Get Comfortable With Being Uncomfortable	119
Chapter 24 Change How You Respond to Failure	122
Chapter 25 Your Thoughts Are Contributing To Your Failure	127
Chapter 26 Don't Take Or Make Failure Personal	129
Chapter 27 It Breaks A Mother's Heart To See Her Child Fail	133
Chapter 28 A FailureTastic Moment	137
Chapter 29 My Daughter's Failure	140
Chapter 30 Potential Failure Is Worth The Risk	142
Chapter 31 Struggle Is Good! I Want To Fly	146

Dedication

This book is dedicated first and foremost to my kids: Sarah, Jacob, Elizabeth, and Rachel. They themselves have faced many challenges at the very early stages of their young lives, but never gave up in the face of their failures. You have taught me that love is unconditional, and for this I thank and love you dearly. You all are the wind beneath my wings.

To my parents, who taught me that struggle is not something we should fear, and that you will get an honest day's pay for an honest day's work. You both did the best that you could given the situation wherein you found yourselves.

Finally, for all of you out there in this great big world who never gave up, even when everything you were striving for and working diligently to achieve never seemed possible. Instead of quitting when all you seemed to know was failure, you continued on with the mission. When others had given up on you, you believed in yourself. Thank you all!

*"Before God's footstool to confess
A poor soul knelt, and bowed his head;
'I failed,' he cried. The Master said,
'Thou didst thy best—that is success!'"
-Anonymous*

*God grant me the serenity
to accept the things I cannot change,
courage to change the things I can,
and wisdom to know the difference.
- Serenity Prayer*

"Like success, failure is many things to many people. With Positive Mental Attitude, failure is a learning experience, a rung on the ladder, a plateau at which to get your thoughts in order and prepare to try again."
- W. Clement Stone

FAILURE noun

fail·ure | \ ˈfāl-yər \

Definition of failure from Merriam-Webster

1(a): failing to perform a duty or expected action (b) a state of inability to perform a normal function

2 (a): lack of success (b) a failing in business

3 (a): falling short-DEFICIENCY one that has failed

SUCCESS noun

suc·cess | \ sək-ˈses \

Definition of success from Merriam-Webster

1(a): degree or measure of succeeding

2(a): favorable or desired outcome (b) the attainment of wealth, favor, or eminence

Acknowledgments

I spent many years as a career Soldier and one critically key component to having a successful career in the Profession of Arms, is having a team of people who make you look good even when you don't deserve it.

To Marissa and Amy Cohen, daughter and mother whose countless hours on the phone and guidance helped me navigate this world of authoring my first book. I simply would have been lost without your commitment and support.

Nicole Vitale, affectionately known as a former perfectionist and LtCol USAF, Ret.Ned Cummings, who were my first time editors for my book. I know I did not make it easy for you but somehow you guys took the words in my book and made them fly off the page and gave life to my thoughts.

Ronda Toll, who introduced me to Ned. God works in mysterious ways. On you last day at work, had you not looked at your email, you would have never introduced me to Ned, and I have no idea where my book or this project might be. We are going to transform the world. I am looking forward to working with you in the future.

Dr. Cate Johnson, a dear friend who has always been there supporting my children and me as we traversed Germany and made ourselves comfortable at your home while enjoying your company. Serving with you and working on the Women Peace and Security Program at European Command was one of the highlights of my tour of duty there. You taught me how failure truly impacts women.

LTC USA, (Ret.) Robert "Bob" Kloecker, Bob, I sincerely miss our in-depth conversations and all the lessons and wisdom you imparted to me. You've always made it easy to talk about success and failure and your honest feedback motivated me, kept me focused, and forced me to look at both sides of every coin regarding failure.

Command Sergeant Major (Ret.), Adrian L. Liptrot, my dear brother. There simply aren't enough words to convey the importance you continue to manifest in my life. As a career Soldier I have always relied heavily on my best Noncommissioned officers. With you; that continues, although in a different capacity the impact is still the same. Whether out of uniform or in uniform you are the ultimate professional and always willing to give me wise counsel. The honesty and clarity you brought to any situation we've ever talked about has always been a compass to my thought process.

Beth and Mangai HoSang, whose continued support and introduction to the Pivot Physical Therapy team gave me more insight into the challenges PT patients experience.

I am convinced that we were all brought together by the powers that be, to construct this much needed message concerning failure and how to change the fallout from negative to positive. Thank you all for traveling along this journey with me. To Be Continued (TBC)!

-George Milton, The Failure Coach

Foreword

My whole life, I have been described as "a perfectionist", "hard-working", and "a real people-pleaser". I relished in these titles. As a student I strove for excellence, both academically and in my extra-curricular activities. In my Senior year of college, I was taking a full 18 credit course load while also serving on two Executive Boards of collegiate organizations, managing an off-campus apartment complex of forty students, and babysitting three children under the age of twelve. I did all of these things to the best of my ability; I was rewarded handsomely for my efforts, winning multiple department awards and making the Dean's List every semester. That's not to say I did everything perfectly, but I performed all of these tasks with vigor and the desire to be seen as one of the most ambitious students in the class of 2012. Of course, there were times that I failed or fell short, and whenever I failed, I felt deflated. Failure was a sign of weakness, and I was certainly *not* weak.

After graduation, I landed my first full-time job at a record label in New York City, which was one of my biggest goals and earliest dreams. I rode the subway to work each day, my heart soaring and still in disbelief that I *made it*. It was also during this time where I realized that failure is a part of the growth process. I made mistakes, and those mistakes had real consequences. I inadvertently let people down with small missteps, or lapses in attention to detail. For a while, I beat myself up over these minor failures, picking apart my performance and punishing myself for being so "stupid". It wasn't until I decided to change my mindset and begin to learn from these mistakes that I truly *grew*.

We are human. We are fundamentally flawed. There is nothing that can prevent us from failing, but we can change the way we look at failure, recalibrate our actions, and become stronger than we ever thought possible. George's book gives you the tools to fix your perspective, make the best out of failure, and use it as a development tactic. I was honored to have worked on this book with George, and I am truly excited for the journey you're about to undertake! Best of luck, and (I sincerely mean this) I hope you fail a little bit along the way.

-Nicole Vitale, Sr. Manager Digital, 300 Entertainment

Preface

"Everything can be taken from a man but one thing: the last of the human freedoms—to choose one's attitude in any given set of circumstances, to choose one's own way."

-Viktor E. Frankl, Austrian neurologist, *Man's Search For Meaning*

One of my earliest memories was of Germany and the Holocaust, (also known as the Shoah), the infamous genocide where Nazi Germany, aided by its collaborators, systematically murdered some six million European Jews—around two-thirds of the Jewish population of Europe—between 1941 and 1945, during World War II.[1]

I cannot pinpoint exactly why Germany and this horrific event was so prominent in my memory as a very young child. I do remember, however, that I was terrified of who and what I thought the German people were. I remember throughout my childhood that for many years I would have nightmares related to the Holocaust where Nazis would chase me as I ran for dear life, afraid that I would be caught. Why would a black kid growing up in rural East Texas, 5,180

---

[1] https:en.wikipedia.org/wiki/The Holocaust

miles and a world far far away, fear a group of people that he had never met nor had any firsthand experiences? Strangely enough, in these dreams, I didn't see myself as black. I just remember being a kid. However, I did see my playmates as being white and identifying as Jewish.

My only connections to the war were a great uncle on my maternal grandmother's side of the family, and my father's affinity for war movies. I never knew my great uncle, and only saw a couple of photos of him in his World War II United States Army uniform some years later. Even at this very moment, as I am writing this prologue, I can still remember seeing this tall, dark, handsome, athletic looking Soldier staring straight back at me from this photo. As I had stated previously, my father liked to watch a lot of war movies--specifically, World War II movies. He also loved a sitcom at the time of my childhood entitled *Hogan's Heroes*. It was an American television sitcom set in a German POW (prisoner of war) camp during World War II. Bob Crane starred as Colonel Robert E. Hogan, coordinating an international crew of allied prisoners running a special operations group from the camp. Werner Klemperer played Colonel Wilhelm Klink, the incompetent commandant of the camp, and John Banner played the bungling sergeant-of-the-guard, Sergeant Hans Schultz.[2] It is probably those movies I watched with my father, coupled with this weekly sitcom, were the major contributing factors in my grueling nightmares. For whatever the reason, call it curiosity or fascination, for many of

---

[2] https://en.wikipedia.org/wiki/Hogan%27s_Heroes

my adolescent years I was intrigued with Germany and the thought of someday visiting a German prisoner of war camp. I would eventually join the Army and get stationed in Germany twice throughout my military career. And yes, I also visited Dachau, the first of the Nazi concentration camps opened in 1933, intended to hold political prisoners.[3]

I specifically remember one recurring nightmare where I was playing with some Jewish kids, we heard German soldiers in the distance marching up the street, getting closer and closer; careless play ended abruptly when out of nowhere came searing explosions and rapid gunfire. The German soldiers began yelling, which resulted in our screaming and panic. As a young child, I had at this time in my life no actual experience in combat, yet in this dream I found myself in what can only be described as a combat zone. As we ran, the soldiers were firing their weapons in defense of themselves while at the same time doing everything in their power to apprehend every single child that they could. In the dream I was running with what little athletic ability I had and with all the energy I could muster, desperately looking for somewhere to hide.

Filled with panic, I finally found a house that had a porch on it. I didn't know if I was in Germany or East Texas -- but what I did know was that my only way to escape was to crawl underneath this house. As I did so, I narrowly evaded what might have been my capture. It was terrifying, because I felt like I was

---

[3] https://en.wikipedia.org/wiki/Dachau_concentration_camp

suffocating from being in a tiny dark space underneath the house, peering through the steps as I watched the Nazis continue to fight and capture the Jewish children, not knowing if the house would cave in on top of me.

The only other option I thought of in this dream was to try to find another place to hide. I would have to expose myself and my hiding place and potentially become captured. This was the point where my dream would typically end. I would always wake up in terror and drenched in sweat in East Texas, far, far away and safe from the dangers of the German soldiers.

As time went on, I was introduced to a book entitled *"Man's Search for Meaning"* by Viktor E. Frankl. Dr. Frankl was an Austrian professor of neurology and psychology. The book chronicles Frankl's life and survival of Auschwitz Concentration Camp during World War II.

In the book, he lays out his day-to-day experiences while living in Auschwitz. He had lost several family members and was himself tortured while witnessing multiple deaths and executions, and was also, on several occasions, himself near death. There are several principles one can gain from Frankl's book, but I want to focus my attention on just two:

First, throughout his imprisonment and suffering, Dr. Frankl discovered meaning in his suffering and a deeper appreciation for his life. Primarily focusing on his future as he assumed he would be liberated from whichever camp he found himself. This was someone whose entire humanity was stripped from him, yet even in such dire straits, he recognized the future purpose, of his life which gave him the ability to survive his captivity, mistreatment, and torturous reality.

Dr. Frankl took notice of two basic mindsets of his fellow prisoners: those who had lost faith, hope and meaning for life, and those who did not let go of those beliefs. Those who looked at their lives in the concentration camp as a challenge to overcome their circumstances often were the ones who survived rather than those who lost sight of the meaning of their lives. One can argue that Dr. Frankl saw his life, experiences and the events surrounding his existence as learning events and not as failures set upon him by outside forces. His suffering ceased to be misery when he gave that pain significance and purpose. Failure ceases to be a disaster when the disappointment we feel from failing can be given meaning and purpose such as learning to overcome a challenge.

Second, we always have a choice. Life is a constant exercise in making choices. There will always be external forces we can't control, but what we *can* control are those internal forces--our response and our attitude. If you can't change your failure or the situation which caused the failure, you have the power to change your attitude towards failure itself.[4]

---

[4]https://en.wikipedia.org/wiki/Man%27s_Search_for_Meaning

F+RR=S
Failure +Right Response = Success

This is a formula I have come up with to remind myself that anytime I fail, if I choose the correct response then it increases my potential for success.

I read somewhere that life is about 10% what happens to you and 90% how one respond. It is with this concept in mind that came up with this formula. As you read this book and anywhere you see the formula F+RR=S, keep that in mind.

Introduction

"If a book about failures doesn't sell, is it a success?"
-Jerry Seinfeld, comedian & television actor

How is it possible that an impoverished kid raised in a small, rural East Texas town, born of two unwed teenagers (neither of whom were educated beyond the 11th grade), end up where I am today? A guy who barely graduated from high school, yet went on to earn four degrees (two of which are Master's level)--one from the largest seminary in the world, Southwestern Baptist Theological Seminary, where I earned 17 hours toward a Doctorate before leaving the program to become an assistant University Professor of Military Science at Northwestern State University of Louisiana, and the other from the United States Army War College.

A former co-host of a local television show with the Parks and Recreation Department in Fort Worth, Texas. An Officer Candidate School Hall of Famer and a retired colonel in the United States Army who had the amazing honor of serving alongside of and leading some of our nation's greatest warriors in peace time and on multiple battlefields.

I am someone who has had the privilege of briefing United States Ambassadors and politicians from foreign nations. Arguably, the United States of America is a great country. Sometimes it feels like a dream, to have been afforded such incredible opportunities - an "American Dream" -- one that so many people chase.

Along my life's journey, which has taken myself and my family to a lot of exciting places, there have also been many disappointments. In fact, the single most important event which began this journey was indeed *failure*! There has been way more failure than I would have admitted in the past, but those days are behind me now, and failure no longer holds a place of misery in my life the way it once did.

It is my hope that after reading this book--no matter where you are from, no matter your social status, the size of your bank account, the location of your zip code, the number of educational degrees you have, the color of your skin, your sexual orientation, no matter what your report cards or grade reports or exams in school read, and no matter what others say about you and how much anyone puts you down and tries to stigmatize you and label you as "not good enough," that you will be able to embrace, learn from, and see failure not as something that limits you, but rather empowers you and allows you to understand that your greatest resource on the path of "Becoming All That You Can Be," is in fact, FAILURE.

The light said to the darkness, "I am because you are." On my way to achieving my successes, I had to fail--a lot! Often, failure feels like darkness, but in my reality, nothing could be further from the truth. Failure became the light that guided me on my path to achieving success over the course of my life. It is my hope that somewhere in these pages you allow failure to lift you from despair and motivate you to not only focus on success as a goal for your life. It is my experience and belief that if one wants to be successful, he or she *must* fail. Allow your failure to be your guiding light as you travel life's paths. Failure Is Not The Problem®, It Is the Beginning of Your Success.

Chapter One

FEAR OF FAILURE

"Feel the fear...and do it anyway!"
-Susan Jeffers

Why do people fear failure? Is it because failure represents a mark of disgrace associated with a specific unfavorable experience in our lives? Perhaps it defines the quality of person one might believe him or herself to be. Is it because failure signifies shame, disgrace, dishonor, disdain, or a blemish on our personhood? For me, it comes down to one word: stigma. It seems to me that if most people were honest, they could see how failure in and of itself isn't necessarily the issue; it's a stigma associated with the failure which creates the problems. Everyone basically knows that they have failed and will, at some point in the future, fail again. So, failure isn't really the problem--it's the stigma aligned with the failure, which attaches itself to our ego.

I often think of a story I read in a book by retired United States General Colin Powell and his co-author, Tony Koltz, *It Worked For Me, In Life and Leadership*. It went something like this: When General Powell was working as a staff assistant to Secretary of Defense Harold Brown during the Carter administration, he had to referee a heated dispute over some obscure issue. He sat there in a conference room full of people, listening as two lawyers debated their points of view. Apparently, one of the lawyers became increasingly personal. As he grew more and more agitated, he got himself tied up in arguments about how the outcome would affect him personally. General Powell said that he lost patience and stopped the debate. He had heard enough. He decided in favor of the other lawyer, based on the strength of his presentation and reasoning. The fellow who "lost" looked crushed, to the discomfort of everyone in the room. The other lawyer looked at him and said, "Never let your ego get so close to your position that when your position falls, your ego goes with it." In short, accept that your position was faulty, not your ego. [5]

For many, it is critical for their friends, their community, their families and colleagues see them in a favorable light. There is absolutely nothing wrong with wanting to be thought highly of and respected.The challenge is, despite how others see you, to recognize how you see yourself, particularly when you fail. Hoping that everyone will like you is setting yourself up for failure. Interesting irony, isn't it? This is a prime example of stimulus and response!

---

[5] Colin Powell and Tony Koltz, *IT WORKED FOR ME, In Life and Leadership.* (10 East 53rd Street, New York, NY 10022, Harper Collins, 2012), page 9.

To find the causes of fear of failure, we first need to understand what "failure" actually means.

We all have different definitions of failure, simply because we all have different values, experiences, and belief systems. A failure to one person might simply be a great learning experience for someone else. Many of us are afraid of failing, at least some of the time. Fear of failure (also called "atychiphobia") is when we allow fear to stop us from doing the things that can move us forward to achieve our goals. Fear of failure can be linked to many causes. For instance, having critical or unsupportive parents is a cause for some people. Because they were routinely humiliated in childhood, people who experienced this lack of support carry those negative feelings into adulthood. Experiencing a traumatic event at some point in your life can also be a cause. For example, say that several years ago you gave an important presentation in front of a large group, and you did very poorly. Because of that poor performance, many teased you about it. The experience might have been so terrible that you became afraid of failing in other things, and you may carry that fear with you even now, years later.

What about those powers of influences outside of your home, such as being told repeatedly by teachers and coaches that you aren't smart, or that the best you can do after graduation is to get a factory job and not ever to think about going to college? Or worse, when you mention that you were thinking about going to college, and the entire room goes silent for a moment, then explodes in laughter? No matter what others may think of you, at the end of the day, you must make a choice. If you find yourself in an unsupportive environment, when all is said and done, how you respond is up to you. The choice is yours.

"Between stimulus and response there is a space. In that space is our power to choose our response. In our response lies our growth and our freedom."

-Viktor E. Frankl, Austrian neurologist

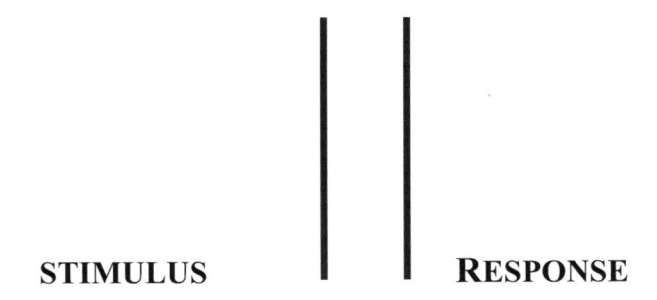

STIMULUS | | **RESPONSE**

Stimulus: an agent (such as a change) that directly influences the activity. Response: something constituting a reply or a reaction.

Your thoughts can determine your outcome. Outside forces may limit your power, but you still hold the power to choose. Focus on your power to choose. Your choices determine your outcomes. You can choose to allow failure to paralyze you, or you can choose to allow failure to teach you and make you better. There are several ways in which we sometimes automatically allow failure to impact our lives:

1. Anger
2. Paranoia
3. Fear
4. Avoidance
5. Depression

A better approach can be to proactively take control of your responses to failure through your thoughts and actions. For example, instead of automatically defaulting to anger, paranoia, fear, avoidance, or depression, choose the opposite views below:

1. Peace
2. Well-Grounded (mindfulness)
3. Trust (of yourself and others)
4. Engagement
5. Vitality (happiness)

There are 86,400 seconds, 1,440 minutes, or 24 hours in a day. How you spend that time is important. Are you going to spend that time worrying about failure and what you haven't accomplished? At the end of the day, how you spend your precious time is your choice. It would be much better spent focusing on the positive aspects of what failure has to offer, rather than the gloom and doom you've previously allowed to rule your life.

That space between stimulus and response, will it be filled in with anger, paranoia, fear, avoidance, or depression? Or will it be replaced with peace, you becoming well-grounded and engaged, and ultimately living a life full of vitality and happiness? Even amid failure, the latter is possible if only you believe and respond accordingly.

"Fear of failure, I thought, will never be our downfall as a company. Not that any of us thought we wouldn't fail; in fact we had every expectation that we would. But when we did fail, we had faith that we'd do it fast, learn from it, and be better for it."

-Phil Knight, Founder of Nike

Chapter Two

SELF-REGULATION

"Success doesn't teach as many lessons as failure does."
-Jay Samit , author

In the Army, we live daily by regulations. We have regulations for almost everything and govern our lives in such a way that those leaders who are serious about making the right decisions study (and sometimes memorize) certain regulations or "regs," as we affectionately refer to them. These regulations establish our missions, responsibilities, and policies; they delegate authority, set objectives, and prescribe mandated procedures to ensure uniform compliance with those policies. These guidelines allow for our military to work and fight and protect our national defense as a team.

Not only is it important to follow and accept the regs, which ensure good order and discipline, it is equally as important to be able to self-regulate. This is true particularly when it's related to failure. It's not that we have failures in our lives that are the concerns, it's how we look at failure and how we allow it to impact our lives. Thinking that you are going to avoid failure by always winning is unrealistic. It's about finding the right balance between winning and failure, which is, in my view, all about attitude. It's about being self-controlled and being able to put into practice positive thoughts and actions, and not defaulting to the belief that failure has no good.

Self-regulation can be defined in various ways. In the most basic sense, it involves controlling one's behavior, emotions, and thoughts in the pursuit of long-term goals. More specifically, emotional self-regulation refers to the ability to manage disruptive emotions and impulses; in other words, to think before acting. It also reflects the ability to cheer yourself up after disappointments and to act in a way that is consistent with your most deeply held values.

Who or what are some of the concerns you need to regulate, remove, re-examine, or rebalance in your life in order to ensure you change the way you relate to failure from a negative to a positive perspective? From my experience, people tend to become more like those they hang around or associate with.

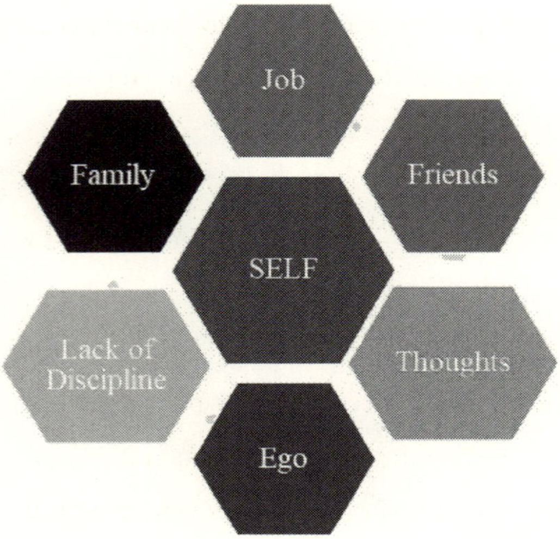
Job
Family
Friends
SELF
Lack of Discipline
Thoughts
Ego

Regulate____

Remove____

Re-examine______________________________________

Rebalance_______________________________________

All we hear about the world over (and this country, specifically) is "win, win, win." We teach our children that if you don't win, you're a loser. If you don't win, you're a failure. That's not necessarily true. What do we really learn if we win? I'm not going to try to answer that question for anyone, but it's something that I believe everyone needs to examine. What do you learn if you lose? Winning isn't bad, but it certainly isn't everything. In the same way, losing isn't the end, but rather it's the *beginning* if you allow it to be. Look at the inner strength one must have in order to be able even to just *try*. We need to allow people to fail. You need to allow yourself to fail. The stigma doesn't have to last forever.

One can grow and move beyond an experience of failure. No one can ask for any better than your best. Give 100% of the best of your ability, and be ok with yourself. I wanted so desperately to become a professional football player as well as an Olympic high jumper when I was younger. I did neither of those things, even though I had a reasonably decent athletic career. I even competed and tied for 3rd place against the greatest high jumper of my day, someone I and most high jumpers wanted to emulate, Dwight Stones. I did not see this as failure. That was a once in a lifetime experience. I learned over time how to self-regulate and rebalance my thoughts and experiences.

Chapter Three

FAILURE IN A MAGICAL PLACE

"The journey of a thousand miles begins with one step."
-St. Francis of Assisi

When I was a kid, I remember hearing of this magical place that lots of people often spoke about. People in my neighborhood who spoke about it made it sound like it was the most amazing place on earth. In this magical land, a person was only limited by their abilities and their imagination. When I was growing up, I had always heard of places of myths. That's exactly what this place sounded like. In this magical land, there were supposedly innovative ways of looking at the world differently. New and developing medical procedures were being engineered along with evolving ways of generating new food crops. There, in this geographical location, a person could learn new languages. Although there were no guarantees, there was a promise that many, if not most, would be able to position themselves to prosper as they moved forward into the future. It was said that just by visiting this place, the knowledge one gained was invaluable. I simply could not believe that such a place on earth existed. One of the stories that really intrigued me was that this dwelling was a great equalizer among the simple, the smart, the rich and the poor. It was heavily male dominated though. Since I am a male, I surmised that this would only work in my favor.

Ninety-nine percent of the people in my neighborhood and from my ethnic background could only dream about going to such a place. Although I desperately wanted to visit there, I was not sure I could even venture to this place because we simply couldn't afford it anyway, having grown up in such abject poverty.

I was told that many people after visiting this place had their dreams realized, but there were also countless others that, no matter how much they tried, they just weren't able to adjust. It wasn't for everyone. I wanted to visit this place. As I grew into maturity, I continued to trust and believe what was told to me because the stories never dissipated, and there were a few people whom I knew personally who had visited there and lived to tell their story. The day came when I had the first of several opportunities to visit there also. I promise, it does exist. All the stories I heard were true. I was shocked and amazed that this place did exist. In fact, I liked it so much that I literally visit there six or seven times. It was like no place I had ever visited. I have visited many countries and places throughout my Army career, but this place was the one location which opened my eyes to many new worlds. Here's the secret, it still exists today. It's called Egelloc. Sorry, I spelled it backwards...College!

This is the list of colleges I attended and failed out of prior to ever receiving a degree of any sort: San Jacinto Jr. College in Deer Park, Texas; Southern Arkansas University in Magnolia, Arkansas; Central Texas College, through the U.S. Army. University of Maryland, through the U.S. Army; Troy State University, through the U.S. Army; Clemson University in Clemson, South Carolina.

F+RR=S

Failure + Right Response = Success

Although I failed out of multiple colleges and universities, I learned how to use those failures to gain more clarity, change how I studied, be more focused and disciplined, and to have more confidence in myself. Those skills I learned through my failures eventually afforded me the opportunity to also earn multiple degrees. My response to the failure was to <u>NEVER GIVE UP</u>!

Chapter Four

BEING UNFIT DOESN'T MEAN BEING UNQUALIFIED

"There is no failure as long as you learn from your experience, continue to work, and continue to press on for success."

-Maya Angelou

Throughout my military career, there were multiple times when I had to explain to a Soldier that he or she wasn't a good fit for the military. It was not always easy to do, but very often necessary because of the responsibilities we have as Soldiers. That being said, I can't ever imagine telling Oprah Winfrey that she is "unfit" for television, like one Baltimore TV producer once did; According to Kathryn Orford's book, *Become Your #1 Fan*, Winfrey was fired from her evening news reporting gig with Baltimore's WJZ-TV because she got too emotionally invested in her stories. The show's producer reportedly told her she was "unfit for television news." As a consolation, however, he offered her a role on a daytime TV show called *People Are Talking*. The show became a hit, and Winfrey stayed on for eight years, according to Biography.com. Winfrey eventually became the host of *The Oprah Winfrey Show*, which aired for 25 seasons.[6]

As a Soldier I advanced fairly quickly up the ranks and received promotions rapidly. Once I achieved the rank of Sergeant, I professionally became a Non-Commissioned Officer (NCO) and thereby a coach, mentor and trainer. The day came where I had to teach my first class. It goes without saying that I was confident but somewhat nervous, though I had done extensive research on my topic. After an hour of intensive lecturing, it was finally over. I was totally motivated, excited, and somewhat exhausted. From what I could tell, the Soldiers were engaged and enjoyed the class. Now, any time training is given by a newly promoted NCO, there's normally a Senior NCO supervising to provide feedback and critique through an apparatus known as an After-Action Review (AAR).

Because the class had gone so well, and all Soldiers were participating, I was ready to receive a *GO* at that station. However, the Senior NCO immediately addressed me by my rank and name which, in the Army, isn't good. He began by saying that I had performed "ok." Well, what could go wrong? I thought, "Well that was the objective, right?" He continued to elaborate that my delivery was good, motivation was superior, training aids and visual aids were sufficient,

---

[6]https://www.inc.com/business-insider/21-successful-people-who-rebounded-after-getting-fired.html

and that I kept the Soldiers engaged and motivated. However, no one could understand anything I had said. As he went on critiquing my training, I grew increasingly confused. If I had performed well, what was the problem? His final analysis was that, although the class went well, my "accent" was so thick that Soldiers had a very difficult time understanding exactly what I was saying.

I grew up in a small, rural area of East Texas called Jacksonville. In this area, we spoke what is known as "Texas English." The dialect is a brand of American English, but with a Southern twist. When you are raised in an environment where everyone basically speaks the same language with the same dialect, it's considered normal and no one is any wiser. When one ventures away from those surroundings, it often times becomes very transparent that others speak a different dialect altogether, and what you consider "normal" speech is quite the opposite. This was my experience to a T.

I was crushed. I had spent countless weeks researching my topic, coordinating the training space, setting up appointments with equipment resources, not to mention I had used up several of my weekends to prepare. As he continued the AAR, my mind went blank. I just could not understand what went so wrong. How could I have possibly failed? Although the NCO never used the word "fail," in my mind, that is exactly what had happened. I had let everyone of my Soldiers down, and worse, I felt that I was a failure in the eyes of those I was trained to lead.

What was I going to do to ensure that Soldiers understood what I was saying when I was leading them? The only way to correct this deficiency was to get some training, so I decided to sign up for speech classes. The rest, as we say in Texas, is history!

F+RR=S
Failure + Right Response = Success

We are in the habit of telling ourselves that failure is bad. Get into the habit of telling yourself that failure is not only good, but necessary. Break one habit and start another.

If you had goals and failed at achieving them, then *dream over, dream again*. At one point, my dream was to become a Senior Non-Commissioned Officer. In order to make this happen, I did not quit. I did not give up. My response to my personal language barrier/failure was to sign up for those speech classes to give myself the advantage I needed in order to achieve the goal I had set forth.

Chapter Five
POVERTY DOESN'T MEAN FAILURE

"Life isn't about finding yourself. Life is about creating yourself."
-George Bernard Shaw

When you're poor, people often expect you to fail. As I've already mentioned, I grew up in extreme poverty. That's neither good nor bad, necessarily -- it was just where I found my beginning. I do not mean to speak negatively of or disrespect my parents, my environment or my upbringing. In fact, I give praise and honor to those two teenagers who gave me life. They absolutely did the best they could given the situation they found themselves. The environment I grew up in was not always perfect; however, my travels throughout the world have shown me that it could have been much worse.

I never fully understood what the creation of my life meant for my parents until one day long into my adulthood. I was looking at my birth certificate, and the first thing I noticed was their ages. My mother was 16 years of age, and my father, 15. The second thing that jumped off the page was their occupations. My mother had no job, as she was, at that time, still a student in high school. My father's occupation as noted on my birth certificate was, "Yard Boy." Even now as I see those two words together, I find it somewhat humorous. They were mere kids when I was born, as well as when my sisters were born. I always saw them through my eyes as adults. They weren't nearly prepared to take on this responsibility of parenthood, but they did it anyway.

Although neither graduated from high school, both of my parents were very hard workers, and actually pretty smart people. They simply lacked the opportunity to achieve many of the dreams they had for themselves and their children. A formal education may not have been the main priority for my parents, but feeding and clothing their three children was just as well as a good education for this child too. Getting that good education was supposed to start with me, their first born. Getting a "good education" in my neighborhood did not necessarily mean getting "educated," but often meant passing to the next grade. Getting that good education, fortunately, started off very slowly. In fact, it began in kindergarten. I actually *failed* kindergarten. I say "fortunately" because this began my first brush with failure in my life. Over the course of many years, there were a multitude of failures along my path to reasonable successes.

Throughout the educational institutions and processes I failed most of my courses, but somehow ended up getting passed along the way. I would always barely pass with lots of D's and the occasional F, but passing was passing, and that meant that as long as I was promoted to the next grade that I was getting a "good education," or so my family and I thought. This came to a screeching halt during my senior year in high school. I had weathered most of the storms thus far and was now about to become the first high school graduate in my family. This was a major feat, given the challenges--financial and otherwise--that we endured as a family and those I had survived as a student. The initial threat to my graduation status came in the way of my high school counselor wanting to talk to me. I arrived at her office and she said to me, "You are not going to graduate on time." I thought, "What the F#@K?" (in those days you could think it, but it was definitely forbidden to say it). I was shocked! Of course, I wanted to know why and how this could have happened. She explained that I was one course hour short of the required credit hours needed to graduate. I immediately petitioned her and said that some of my teachers had been willing to help in the past and would perhaps be willing to do so now so that I may graduate. She made it clear that those days of extended help were over. She went on to explain that I could and would graduate; however, that would be during the summer after I took a summer class, which also meant that I would not be walking across the stage along with my graduating class. I was the only football player on our team to make the first team all-district line up, the best record-setting pole vaulter in the history of our school who advanced to the state track and field meet, the best record-setting high jumper ever in the history of our high school, and competed on multiple relays and races for the school. I thought surely, there was at least one teacher who would have sympathy for me and would be enticed to "help a brother out." Nope! My counselor wasn't having it. That was that! Case closed.

I was in sheer panic mode. How was I going to tell my parents? *What* was I going to tell my parents? How could I face them? Once again, "failure" had reared its ugly head, as it often had throughout my life. There had to something that could be done in order to help me graduate on time. I wanted to walk across that stage with my parents in the audience, watching their pride and joy in all of his glory. I petitioned my counselor for weeks on end, sometimes becoming so emotional I broke down crying uncontrollably. Most of those conversations ended with her saying she was sorry, but there was nothing more she could do.

Then one day I was unexpectedly called to her office. I had no idea what was about to take place, but it would be life changing. As I walked into her office she was smiling. She motioned for me to take a seat, and she began to explain that she had figured something out and had come up with a plan for me to graduate on time. All I could think was, "Thank you, Jesus, thank you Jesus, *thank you Jesus*!" and I was so overjoyed. I figured that she had obviously spoken with my teachers and petitioned one who was willing to give me a passing grade so that I could graduate on time. Or, maybe one of my teachers had cornered her and petitioned her, and suggested a passing grade. At this point I didn't care; all I heard was that I would be graduating on time and walking across that stage with my classmates.

She began by stating that she had gotten permission to order a correspondence course for me to take. My joy turned into confusion. "A *what* course ma'am?" I asked. Correspondence? I couldn't even spell correspondence, let alone have any earthly idea what it meant. She explained that it was a self-taught course where I would take the course material, read through it on my own, and afterwards take a test. If I passed the test, I would graduate on time. I thought that seemed simple enough. What a relief! Of course, there is a phrase that goes something like, "When something seems too good to be true, it usually is." Well, this was just that.

She explained that the correspondence course was in a subject called Botany. As I sat there, a look of confusion must have blanketed my face, and she began to describe that it was the study of plants. She also mentioned that the course was from Stephen F. Austin State University in Nacogdoches, Texas. I reminded her that I was a failing high school student. What were the chances of me actually passing this course? This information, as Yoda would say, "returned my anguish, it did"!

So here I am, a failing high school student (trying to become the first high school graduate in his family), and the path to that one goal is through a correspondence course in a hard science at a University level. What were the odds? In that moment, I figured it was good that I had gotten somewhat used to failing. I took the course material home and over a couple weeks I muddled through it, not learning much of anything. I took the exam, returned the material to my counselor, and after a couple more weeks the material was returned to my school. My counselor called me into her office where we opened the results letter together. I had absolutely no expectation of passing that course. I don't know who was more nervous, me or my counselor. As she was reading, I didn't see her smile and I immediately felt that I would not be graduating on time. Without any expression, she handed me the letter. The disappointment I felt was overwhelming. "Failure again," I thought. As I struggled through the paperwork trying to find the grade, I fought back tears. Finally, there it was," a D. I questioned out loud, "...a D?", to which she smiled and said," Yes. Congratulations, you passed!" There were two things I did at that moment -- 1, I became deluged with happiness, and 2, I thought, "At least I'm consistent by getting a D."

F+RR=S

Failure + Right Response = Success

It matters not where we start; what's important is the life we create for ourselves. My response to the hardships and those challenges I began life with was to not allow poverty and repeated failures determine my outcome in life. In Jack Canfield's book, *The Success Principles: How to Get from Where You Are to Where You Want to Be*, principle #17 is ASK! ASK! ASK!....In other words, become an ASK hole! I don't know if it was divine intervention, the Law of Attraction, or simply my counselor being tired of me asking, but it worked.

Chapter Six

FAILURE IS ABOUT SELF-REFLECTION

Pessimist: "Oh, this can't get any worse!"
Optimist: "Yes, it can!"
-Bharat Jakati

There were many times throughout my life when I was exhausted and just wanted to give up. Nothing seemed to go the way I wanted it to. People quit on me, and I felt abandoned. Sure, people *will* quit on you; sometimes people *will* abandon you. Unfortunately, there are times when this happens more often than we'd like it to. The good news is, as much as we would like to believe that this matters, it doesn't! What really matters is that *YOU* never give up on *YOU*. At the end of the day, you're the only one who can let yourself down. Don't quit on *YOU*!

In the Army, we teach Soldiers to live the Warrior Ethos which states:

"*I will always place the mission first. I will never accept defeat. I will never quit. I will never leave a fallen comrade.*"

An Ethos is a set of beliefs on which a person or group decides to live by. What is your personal Ethos when it comes to failure? Regardless of my situation, I get to choose what my beliefs and ideas are regarding failure, and the best part is, so do you. Try this one on for size:

Failure Ethos:
Always believe in yourself.
Never accept that you are defeated.
Never stop moving forward.
Never lower your standards to measure up to other people's standards.
Never leave yourself behind.
Never ever, ever, give up on yourself!

There are many reasons I failed in the past. Everyone has different reasons, and recognizing those reasons through self-reflection is important. Use these moments of self-reflection to determine what is holding you back and allowing failure to become a negative force in your life. Here are a few common doorways to failure that people allow to drag them down:

1. Poor Self-Esteem

Poor self-esteem is a lack of self-respect and self-worth. Everyone has flaws, but you should never think of yourself as less-than or not worthy. Although you have failed, you're not a failure until you stop trying.

2. Lack of Discipline

I would argue that most people who have accomplished anything worthwhile have never done it without some measure of discipline. Discipline takes self-control, sacrifice, and avoiding distractions and temptations. Discipline requires staying focused. This is a code by which Soldiers must live.

3. Attitude

As a Soldier, I've learned that people usually meet the standards that are set for them, whether they are high or low. One of the major determining factors has always been their attitude. Thus, attitude determines altitude.

4. Rationalization

Rationalization is the act of attempting to explain or justify a behavior or a mindset with logical reasons, even if they are inappropriate or don't make sense. For example: once an enemy combatant drops or lays down his weapon, he is considered a Prisoner of War (POW) by American military rules, laws and standards. To treat the POW as anything otherwise goes against our training and no amount of rationalization will hold up, even in a court of law.

5. Never Starting

"Even the longest and most difficult ventures have a starting point" - Proverb

Understanding and admitting your reasons for failing can be empowering. Can you identify the reasons you've failed? Don't limit your responses or answers. Fill in the bottom diagram.

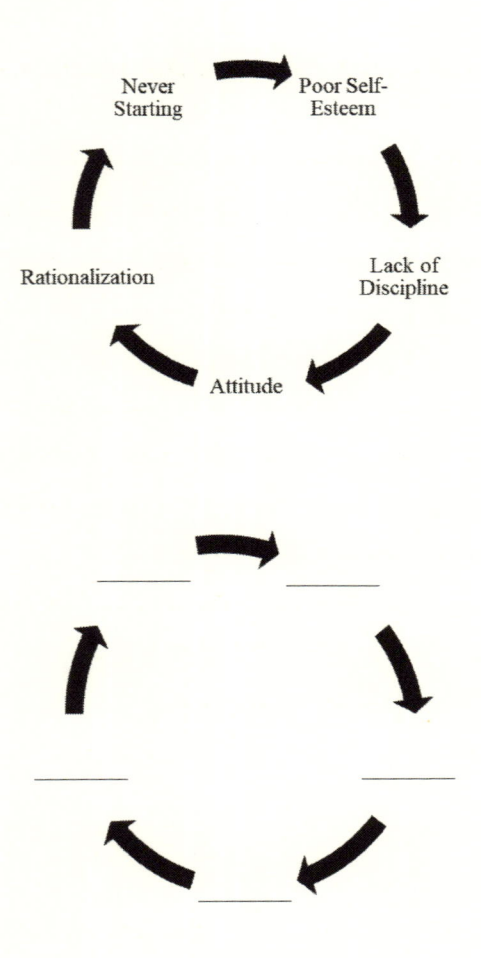

Never Starting → Poor Self-Esteem → Lack of Discipline → Attitude → Rationalization → (Never Starting)

_____ → _____

_____   _____

_____

Chapter Seven

<u>FEAR OF FAILING MIGHT GET YOU ON TV</u>

"A young boy enters a barber shop and the barber whispers to his customer, 'This is the dumbest kid in the world. Watch while I prove it to you'. The barber puts a dollar bill in one hand and two quarters in the other, then calls the boy over and asks, 'Which do you want, son?'. The boy takes the quarters and leaves.
'What did I tell you?' said the barber. 'That kid never learns!'
Later, when the customer leaves, he sees the same young boy coming out of the ice cream parlor. 'Hey, son! May I ask you a question? Why did you take the quarters instead of the dollar bill?'
The boy licked his cone and replied, 'Because the day I take the dollar the game is over!
-- Vinaya Patil

When you don't succeed, make sure that your failures are your own, and not failures from the expectations of others. Media personality Steve Harvey shared a story on an Oprah Winfrey Network (OWN) episode about how he wanted to be on television. When his father (who was nicknamed "Slick") came home, he was informed by Steve's mother that Steve was at school being a smart aleck. Steve said that he already knew that he was going to get a whipping for that behavior, and he was told to share with his dad what he had written on a sheet of paper while in class. On the paper was Steve's dream that he wanted to be on television. His dad asked what was so wrong with what he had written down. Steve's mom said that Steve was being a smart-aleck by putting something so unbelievable for someone of his background on that sheet of paper. Perhaps one of the concerns Steve's mom had was the fact that he had a stuttering problem. His dad argued that it was fairly reasonable for Steve to have written this down. The conversation continued to the point to where an argument between his parents started brewing. At this point, Steve was told to go to his room, which meant in his mind that he was about to get the anticipated whipping.

Steve went to his room and, after his parent's discussion, his dad came to him and asked, "What does she (the teacher) want you to put on your paper?" Young Steve said, "I don't know daddy, like a basketball player, like what all the rest of the kids wrote." His dad told Steve to write what the teacher wanted on the piece of paper, then take that sheet of paper to school the following day and give it to the teacher. Then his dad instructed Steve to take his original sheet of paper with his dream of being on TV written on it and put it in his drawer. He said, "Every morning when you get up, read your paper. Every night before you go to bed, read your paper. That's your paper!" Steve said that what his father taught him was a principle of success. If you write your goal down and envision it, anything you see in your mind, you can hold in your hand.

When Steve became an adult, he made it a point every year while his former teacher was alive to send her a TV for Christmas, because he wanted her to see him on TV. By the way, he kept the paper long after his time at that school. That little boy with the stuttering problem is currently on TV seven days a week.[7]

This is a fantastic story of personal success, of course, but there are other lessons as well. "Slick" (Steve's father) in his infinite wisdom did not allow stereotypes to limit his son. All his teacher and outsiders could see were limitations and failure. What if they could have simply been wise enough to understand that even if he had tried and failed, he would have perhaps learned a very valuable lesson about setting goals and striving for those goals? One can make the argument that they were merely trying to protect young Steve. Unfortunately, and often unintentionally, this is how it is ingrained in our society how unacceptable failure is amongst those who have our best intentions in mind.

Another lesson was that his daddy understood the importance of not only writing something down and envisioning it, but he also knew that, given his and

---

[7] I transcribed this from YouTube of an old episode of Oprah Winfrey Network as she interviews Mr. Harvey.

his son's background, that achieving such a lofty goal was not going to be an easy task and would involve some failure. Instead of telling Steve to forget about this dream of being on TV and focus on something that seemed more "natural" or more "realistic" in the eyes of others, his father supported young Steve and allowed room for the possibility of failure, while at the same time not focusing solely on his son's potential success. He remained neutral, yet supportive. I bet that if we could ask Steve Harvey--along with finding a way to get on TV-- if he had any other fears of failing and wondered if this goal would become a reality, there would be at least one "Yes." Maybe someday I will be able to ask him that exact question!

The final lesson to be learned from this story is to never allow anyone to define who you are. You are responsible for deciding who you are, and who you will become. It is your choice to embrace, accept, or reject your successes and your failures. The trick is to remember that success and failure are two sides of the same coin. They both have value. What you do with that coin or where you spend it is up to you!

"For me failure is not failure-it's a valuable learned gained experience."
-- Steve Harvey

Chapter Eight

__CHANGE YOUR MINDSET, BE DISCIPLINED__

"Anything worth doing is worth doing badly until you get it right."
-Les Brown, Motivational Speaker

Barring any physical ailments and assuming one has a solid mental stability, my experiences have shown me that when it comes to failure, it's mainly about mindset. In order to prepare your mindset to think of failure as a positive experience instead of a negative one, you must be self-disciplined. Once you change your mindset and your attitude, it becomes easier. Not *easy*, but *easier*. Most people want easy. Easy is not the goal; training the mind and becoming more disciplined is. My experience has been that those things, which I've had to work the hardest for, are the events I've appreciated and have learned the most from.

I failed a lot in school, so for me it was normal not to understand the value of failure. Although that was my reality, the teachers I remembered most and respected most, and really appreciated (specifically, my coaches), were the ones who were the hardest on me. They didn't give me a pass. They made me work for those failing grades. I failed, but I learned from that failure also. It taught me that a letter grade wasn't the point. I've had several coaches who come to mind when I think about which of them were the hardest on me. One coach rises to the top: A short, burly, barrel chested, bulldog faced, former Marine named Wade Williams. In fact, coach Williams was the first Marine I had any real experience with. By the time we met, I had already served in the Army for a few years, so I understood the importance of being disciplined. Coach Williams took discipline to a whole different level. He recruited me out of the Army and brought me to Clemson University where I competed as a high jumper and a decathlete. I was always an athlete, and since I had served in the Army for a while, I knew discipline and I knew pain.

The specific event I will attempt to relay to you was this: Coach Williams wanted me and my teammates to gain strength in our legs and buttocks, as well as lung capacity for endurance. He brought out something I had never seen before. It was something like a snow sled made of sheet metal, with rubber tubing attached to it in such a way that it reminded me of what I used to see when I was growing up in Texas. Imagine, if you will, a miniature stagecoach. I remember riding on horse-driven wagons that my family used to ride in on our way to horse races on Sundays after church. This contraption was similar, except that it had no wheels. It looked like something one would ride down a snow capped mountain. Coach Williams separated the runners from the jumpers. We stood around looking at one another in bewilderment and confusion, asking what the heck this contraption was. Coach approached us. He called one of the high jumpers over. He took this harness (which was attached to the rubber tubing), jumped on the sled and said to the athlete, "Run until I say stop." But the way, it's about 85 degrees, typical hot South Carolina weather on a grass covered field -- no snow to be found within a thousand miles. As our teammate ran as hard and as fast as he could--about 40 meters down and 40 meters back to the starting point--the rest of us looked on with thoughts of amazement, confusion and sudden confidence. Now our competitive spirits kicked in. At this point we all wanted to try, especially yours truly.

I wanted to have the fastest time down and back. I'm strapped in the harness. This bulldog-looking, stubby former Marine hops onto the sled, blows his whistle and I take off with every ounce of strength I can muster. It was about 10 meters into his blissful ride and my torment and agony that what seemed to be simply another training was something that required tremendous discipline over time to get the results he wanted. Day after day, we failed for weeks until we changed our mindset from seeing those failures to understanding that this one exercise went from being mental anguish to mind over matter. Eventually, it was just another intense exercise which increased our speed and the strength of our jumps. I was now easily high jumping seven plus feet in the high jump and completing races with even faster times than before. It took a while, but eventually we finally got it right.

If you really want to turn your failures into success, it's all about changing your mindset. For one to change their mindset, they must be committed to discipline.

D- Devoted

I- Inspired

S- Strong

C- Courageous

I- Intuitive

P- Patient

L- Lazy, one must not be

I- Insistent

N- Never quit

E- Energized

$$F+RR=S$$

Failure + Right Response = Success

My response to what appeared to be prolonged failure was to look at my experiences from a different perspective--to look at my experiences as positive rather than negative.

Chapter Nine
FAMOUS PEOPLE ALSO FAIL

"Trying is the first step towards failure."

-Homer Simpson

The standard of success tends to be celebrities.

Famous people who failed, but went on to make a difference in the world:

1. _____ Failed in business three times and failed campaigning seven times prior to becoming President of the United States.

2. _____ Wasn't able to speak until he was four years old. His parents thought he was "subnormal." He was also expelled from school and his teachers described him as mentally slow.

3. _____ Was cut from his high school basketball team for having no skill.

4. _____ A Harvard University dropout and his first business, Traf-O-Data was a failure.

5. _____ Although his teachers told him he was too stupid to learn anything, after 1000 failures, he went on to light up the world.

6. _____ When he was 30 years old, he was left devastated and depressed after being fired from the company he started.

7. _____ Although her life looks much different today, she had a rough start. She had a very difficult and abusive childhood and was actually fired from her job because she was "unfit for TV."

8. _____ They were rejected by Decca Recording Studios and were told that the geniuses at the record label "did not like their sound" and that they "had no future in show business."

9. _____ She was dropped by 20th Century Fox movie studios after one year because her producer told her that she wasn't pretty or talented enough to be an actress.

10. _____ He was fired from a newspaper for "lacking imagination" and having "no original ideas."

11. _____ He was a failure at three businesses before finally succeeding at the ripe old age of 53. In his day, he would have been considered past his prime. Age never has to be what determines whether you will succeed in life. Imagine all the knowledge and wisdom one can get from living beyond your twenties and thirties...

12. _____ None other than the Colonel himself. Early on, he couldn't even sell chicken. This chicken shack is one of the most recognizable chicken restaurants on the planet.

13. _____ His first book, *Carrie* was rejected 30 times. He almost threw the book in the trash, which potentially could have been the career ender of someone that a lot of people would argue is the most prolific horror writer ever.

14. _____ An engineer and industrialist who was quoted as saying; "Success is 99 percent failure." The founder of a leading Motor Company who developed a piston ring early in his life that he wanted to sell to another Automotive Company. It is reported that he took the design to Toyota who told him that his work was not up to their standards.

15. _____ She was an unemployed, divorced mother raising a daughter on social security while writing her first fantasy novel. The novel was rejected by 12 publishing housing. Apparently, those who passed on her initial book proved Dumbledore's statement to be true: "You fail to recognize that it matters not what someone is born, but what they grow to be."

16. _____ The Law School Admission Test (LSAT) is an essential part of law school admissions in the United States. This test is designed specifically to assess key skills needed for success in law school, including reading comprehension, analytical reasoning, and logical reasoning. She failed it twice but went on to become a billionaire providing Booty-Lusciousness.

17. _____ In his early 30's, he started the first Nylon and Velcro surfer wallet businesses, but went broke. He lost $800,000.00 at 32 years of age. He was homeless at one point, but to date is worth $80, 000,000.00.

What do all these people have in common? One, they all went on to be at least moderately successful. Two, they all failed. Three, none of them allowed failure to stop them from reaching their goals and dreams.

Answer to Famous people who failed but went on to make a difference in the world quiz:

1. Abraham Lincoln
2. Albert Einstein
3. Michael Jordan
4. Bill Gates
5. Thomas Edison
6. Steve Jobs
7. Oprah Winfrey
8. The Beatles
9. Marilyn Monroe
10. Walt Disney
11. Henry Ford
12. "Colonel" Harland Sanders (KFC)
13. Stephen King
14. Soichiro Honda
15. J.K. Rowling
16. Sara Blakey
17. Robert Kiyosaki

Celebrities with learning disabilities

1. Keira Knightley - (Dyslexia)

Diagnosed with dyslexia at age six, *Pirates of the Caribbean* star Keira Knightley has said her struggles with reading at an early age only made her tougher. Knightley's mother told her that she could only act if she read every day during the holidays and kept her grades up. With her dream of acting now on the line, she wouldn't be stopped. In her own words: " I drove myself into the ground trying to get over dyslexia and when I finished school, I had the top grades," proving that perseverance is key.

2. Orlando Bloom - (Dyslexia)

Best known for his role as Will Turner in *Pirates of the Caribbean*, Bloom was diagnosed with dyslexia at age seven. Despite his mother's best efforts in getting him to read more, Bloom's struggles left him looking for a creative outlet, so he turned to the stage. He eventually mastered reading out loud in drama school, and even turned his dyslexia to his advantage. "The gift of dyslexia was that I learned everything forward and backward, inside out, so I was fully prepared," he said. "I had to learn everything so that I wouldn't have stage fright, or the lines wouldn't fall out of my mind."

3. Michael Phelps- (ADHD)

Growing up, champion swimmer Michael Phelps was continually criticized by teachers for his inability to sit still and was formally diagnosed with ADHD when he was in fifth grade. After being on Ritalin for over two years, Phelps chose to stop using the drug and instead used swimming to help him find focus. His choice clearly paid off, as he ended his Olympic career as the most highly decorated Olympian of all time, boasting 22 medals (18 of them being gold).

4. Daniel Radcliffe - (Dyspraxia)

Most notable for his role as Harry Potter, Daniel Radcliffe has lived with a mild case of dyspraxia for his entire life. Dyspraxia is a common neurological disorder that affects motor skill development, meaning that at 25 years old and the star of one of the largest franchises in movie history, Radcliffe still has trouble tying his shoelaces. In an interview regarding his Broadway debut, he once jokingly stated, "I sometimes think, Why, oh why, has Velcro not taken off?"

5. Whoopi Goldberg - (Dyslexia)

Actress, writer, and producer Whoopi Goldberg was actually called "dumb" while growing up due to her dyslexia. "I knew I wasn't stupid, and I knew I wasn't dumb. My mother told me that," she said in a 2004 interview. With leading roles in movies like *Sister Act*, *The Color Purple*, and *Jumping Jack Flash*, and being one of the only ten people to win an Emmy, a Grammy, an Oscar, and a Tony Award; She has certainly proven her critics wrong.

6. Steven Spielberg - (Dyslexia)

Indiana Jones, *E.T.*, *Saving Private Ryan*, and *Jurassic Park* are just a few of the movies that legendary filmmaker Steven Spielberg is responsible for. Despite being diagnosed with dyslexia at age sixty, Spielberg struggled with it his entire life. He learned to read two years after all of his classmates and was bullied so much that he dreaded going to school. He offers this advice to students and young adults with learning disabilities, "You are not alone, and while you will have dyslexia for the rest of your life, you can dart between the raindrops to get where you want to go. It will not hold you back."

7. Jamie Oliver - (Dyslexia)

Celebrity Chef Jamie Oliver has authored over twenty cookbooks, and currently holds the title of world's richest chef, with a net worth of over $230 million. With that in mind, it might surprise you to learn that he only finished reading his first book in 2013. He was quoted as saying "I've never read a book in my life, which I know sounds incredibly ignorant but I'm dyslexic and I get bored easily." What did he choose as his first book to finish? *Catching Fire*, the sequel to *The Hunger Games* by Suzanne Collins.

8. Ty Pennington - (ADHD)

Ty Pennington is, in his own words,"about as ADHD as you can get." The former host of ABC's *Extreme Makeover: Home Edition* had a great deal of trouble in school. "I mean, I was so out of control that I spent most of the time in the hallway or in detention," he said. Pennington was formally diagnosed with Attention Deficit Hyperactivity Disorder as an undergrad, and taking the prescribed medication was followed by an immediate upturn in his grades, to the point where he was getting straight A's.

9. Keanu Reeves - (Dyslexia)

Star of *The Matrix* trilogy, *Point Break*, *Bill and Ted's Excellent Adventure*, and most recently *John Wick*, Keanu Reeves' dyslexia caused him to struggle in school. In an interview with *Handbag Magazine* he said, "Because I had trouble reading, I wasn't a good student and I didn't finish high school. I did a lot of pretending as a child. It was my way of coping with the fact that I didn't really feel like I fit in." His gift for pretending has served him well in his acting career, which is still going strong after 30 years.

10. Charles Schwab - (Dyslexia)

Due to his struggle with undiagnosed dyslexia, Charles Schwab bluffed his way through his early years of schooling by reading Classic Comic Book versions of books like *Ivanhoe* and *A Tale of Two Cities*. While attending Stanford University, Schwab was initially floundering, failing both Freshman English and French. "To sit down with a blank piece of paper and write was the most traumatic thing that had ever faced me in life," he admitted. At 77 years old, businessman and investor Charles Schwab has a net worth in excess of $5.1 billion, and yet still finds reading and writing tedious.

11. Paul Orfalea - (Dyslexia and ADHD)

Paul Orfalea struggled the entire way through school due to being unable to focus read properly, which even lead to his expulsion from four of the eight schools he attended. In the end, Orfalea graduated high school with a 1.2 GPA and went on to attend the University of Southern California. While still only getting C's and D's in college, he was working part time on a business venture he called Kinko's. In an interview, he attributed his success in part to his conditions: "My learning disability gave me certain advantages, because I was able to live in the moment and capitalize on the opportunities I spotted."

12. Jay Leno - (Dyslexia)

Jay Leno is a man of many talents: he is a comedian, actor, writer, producer, voice actor and former television host of NBC's *The Tonight Show*. Leno's dyslexia has led him to become a firm believer in low self-esteem: "If you don't think you're the smartest person in the room and you think you're going to have to work a little harder, and put a little more time into it to get what everybody else does, you can actually do quite well. And that's been my approach." His approach to dyslexia has clearly paid off.

12. Sir Richard Branson - (Dyslexia)

Entrepreneur, billionaire, and "the only person in the world to have built eight billion-dollar companies from scratch in eight different countries," Sir Richard Branson is a model for success, who is also dyslexic. Unlike many who consider dyslexia a curse, Branson calls it his "greatest strength." Growing up in a time when dyslexia was largely misunderstood, Branson's teachers simply labeled him as "lazy" or "not very clever." After starting up a successful alternative newspaper in high school, he was confronted by his headmaster who said, "Congratulations, Branson. I predict that you will either go to prison or become a millionaire." Looking back on the incident Branson said, "That was quite a startling prediction, but in some respects he was right on both counts!"

13. Anderson Cooper - (Dyslexia)

A well-known journalist and CNN TV personality, Anderson Cooper has struggled with a mild case of dyslexia from a very early age. Cooper's family placed heavy importance on reading and hired a special reading instructor in order to help him. Cooper persevered by finding books that he was incredibly passionate about, including Helen Keller's biography and Graham Greene's novel *The Quiet American*. While speaking at the National Center for Learning Disability's annual luncheon in 2010, he said, "Luckily I went to a school that caught the problem very quickly and was able to figure out the problem and diagnose it, and luckily I had access to people who could really help."

14. David Neeleman - (ADHD)

JetBlue CEO David Neeleman has turned his ADHD to his advantage, using it to help him focus on the things that he is passionate about. In an interview with *Attitudemag*, Neeleman said, "If someone told me you could be normal or you could continue to have your ADD, I would take ADD." In this spirit, Neeleman refuses to take medication to treat the condition. "I'm afraid of taking drugs once, blowing a circuit, and then being like the rest of you." Instead of allowing his ADD to derail his thoughts, he uses the condition to find more streamlined methods of accomplishing his tasks.[8]

---

[8]: https://www.special-education-degree.net/25-famous-people-with-learning-disorders/

Chapter Ten

YOUR ATTITUDE TOWARD FAILURE IS IMPORTANT

"The secret of getting ahead is getting started. The secret of getting started is breaking your complex, overwhelming tasks into small manageable tasks, then starting on the first one."

-Mark Twain

When it comes to failure, your attitude often determines your outcome. It is important for you to examine your failures and not only why they happen, but also how they impact you. Do not merely go through the motions after you have failed. Use the chart below to check your attitude on how failure impacts your attitude:

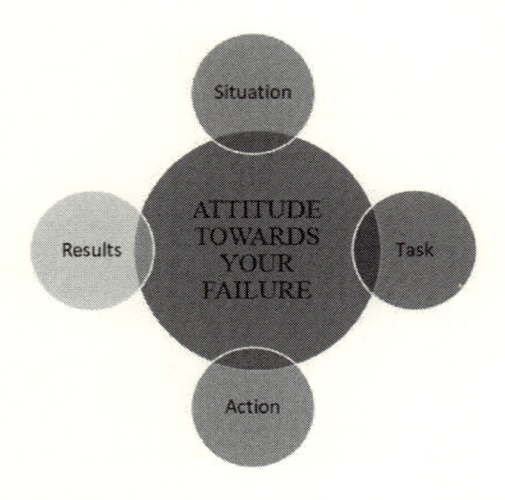

S - Situation: What was the framework you were operating in during the event? Include the challenge or opportunity you faced.

T - Task: What was your objective?

A - Action: What steps did you take in trying to accomplish your goal?

R - Results: What impact did this have on you?

S_____
_____
_____

T_____
_____
_____

A_____
_____
_____

R_____
_____
_____

ATTITUDE TOWARDS YOUR FAILURE:

Ultimately, your ATTITUDE determines your ALTITUDE.

Chapter Eleven

FAILURE UNACCEPTABLE-ONLY WIN

"I never lose. I either win or learn."
-Nelson Mandela

Is it better to win or to fail? Why limit it to two choices? The better goal should be to learn. As I was driving on Interstate 295 North in Richmond, Virginia, a car passed me. I looked at the license plate, as I often do. It read: "ONLY WIN." There is no such thing as "always winning." When you tell yourself that the only option is winning, that's absolutely unrealistic and you're setting yourself up for--you guessed it--failure.

There's nothing wrong with winning, but there's also nothing wrong with failing. You can have an angry, unsatisfied winner or a gracious failure. You may be familiar with the quote, "It's not whether you win or lose, but how you play the game." In playing the game, one objective could be winning; another could be failing, but the correct response whether you win of fail should be learning. What I find interesting about failure is that children have no concept of failure until they are taught that concept. Every child I have ever known (myself included) when faced with a challenge or an obstacle, normally did one or two things: they either figured out a way to meet that challenge and overcame that obstacle, or they made a decision to do something else because they lost interest. What they typically did *not* do was call themselves a failure; at least not until that idea was introduced to them. We were never born to be "failures," whatever that means.

There is someone out there who has either been told they were not good enough, and that they have failed; that they didn't meet the standard. If you haven't been told that, just wait--it's coming. Unless you're a perfect person, you are going to miss a target now and again. That being said, only *YOU* get to decide whether you're a failure or not. *YOU* decide! Just because someone calls you a failure doesn't make you a failure. By the way, where did the word failure come from anyway? The short answer is, men made it up. Sometimes we don't know the answer to a question because we never ask the question in the first place.

I recently watched a 2019 biographical drama entitled, *The Professor and the Madman* starring Mel Gibson and Sean Penn. Based upon a true story, professor James Murray (played by Gibson) was commissioned by aristocrats in 1857 to begin leading and overseeing a committee to compile the *Oxford English Dictionary*. Murray worked with W.C. Minor (played by Penn), a doctor who at the time was institutionalized at a Criminal Lunatic Asylum submitted over

10,000 words to the dictionary.[9] Together and with the help of others, they wrote down words and gave those words definitions. There was no magic to it, no "hallelujah" moment or great awakening. It was simply people deciding what designator a word should have. I am not suggesting that they are the individuals who gave a negative meaning to the word failure. My point is this: it's just a made-up word with a depressing connotation. You get to choose how you use that word, feel about that word, and understand that single word, be it negative or positive.

Simply because you didn't make the team, or didn't get selected, or didn't get that job you've been wanting, or get that pay raise, or were rejected for any number of reasons, that doesn't make you a failure. You simply did not accomplish one of your goals. You may even call it a dream that wasn't achieved. As long as you're still breathing, you can readjust, start over, dream again, find other positions equal to or greater than the one you didn't get. Remember, it's up to *YOU*! The issue is how you see your failures. How do you respond to these failures? What did you learn about the experience and other people you encountered throughout this process? Most importantly, what did you learn about yourself?

---

[9] https://en.wikipedia.org/The_Professor_and_the_Madman_(film).

Your perspective on failure, your relationship with failure, and your understanding of failure is critical in being able to accept failure. *Failure is not the problem®. It's the beginning of your success*. Only *YOU* decide if you are a failure, no one else!

Chapter Twelve

FAILURE IS THE BIG ELEPHANT

"I've never played stupid to keep someone distant. I don't play stupid. Either it's been a failure on my part to articulate, or my naivete, or ingenuousness, or sometimes it's the nature of the form."

-Keanu Reeves

Why do people believe that the rich and powerful are always smarter and wiser? I imagine most people believe that because of their bank accounts, the homes they live in, the cars they drive, the places they travel to for vacations, etcetera. I have often wondered, "What if we tried an experiment?" Let's take a person who is proven to be a very smart person (perhaps a genius), dress them up in unappealing clothing, with mangled hair and poor hygiene, and explain to a passersby that this individual hasn't a penny to their name. Later, we take this same person with the same information and clean them up. Tailored, professional clothing that tops the best of any Fortune 500 company CEO. Expertly and meticulously groomed. Then it's mentioned that the individual is a billionaire. If this person was to present a speech on a revolutionary, world changing idea, who do you think would be more likely to be listened to?

If we are truly honest with ourselves, I think we know who people are more prone to listen to. Why is that? There are probably many answers for many different reasons, but for sure one answer is conditioning. As it is the case with failure, it seems that we too often have been taught, or it's been exampled to us, that failure is unacceptable. I am living proof that failure is good, if looked at in the correct perspective. Maybe the rich and powerful are not any smarter or wiser. Perhaps they simply work harder and have a different, *positive* relationship with failure.

Failure is ubiquitous, right? There is no place on this planet where you can go where failure doesn't exist. It's inescapable. No matter what anyone tells you, failure is and will always be an option because failure, unlike success, is guaranteed, whether you want it to be or not. Failure is an equal opportunity situation. Failure encompasses all generations. Failure is universal. It knows no race, color, creed, gender, class or social status, country, or limits; It hits everyone.

Failure is the kind of experience that captures the imaginations of all kinds of people, from all backgrounds. It is no respecter of person. It doesn't matter who someone is, he or she will suck at something and all of us will fail multiple times. Allow failure to propel you into greatness and be all that you were meant to be. Stop pretending to be someone you were never meant to be. When we fail, others get to benefit from our failure, thus potentially making the world a better, more efficient place.

Chapter Thirteen
<u>FAILURE IS ABOUT RETRAINING</u>

"Success is not final, failure is not fatal: it is the courage to continue that counts."
-*Winston Churchill*

What do you do when others fail you? How do you feel, how do you respond? Their failure can also be your success. I came from a family where alcoholism was infused within my culture. We didn't call it alcoholism, we were just told that Uncle Joe or Uncle Bill or cousin Sally Belle just drank too much. What if, because of societal reasons and inequalities, your parents or caregivers didn't provide for the family? Not that it was easy, but I actively decided that I would change those paradigms. I made a conscience decision to retrain myself in the way I thought, choices I made, and how I responded to so many failures.

I remember telling myself that I was going to break the cycle I was raised in. The first thing I did was accept myself, my family, my environment and my upbringing. No longer was I going to feel sorry for myself and question why I was brought into that particular atmosphere. I couldn't change where I was born, how I was born, or the conditions in which I was born. I embraced my existence.

The second thing I did was to stop blaming God for putting me in my family, and stop blaming my parents for, what I thought at the time was, failing me. Once I became a parent, I understood that my teenage parents did the best they could, given their situation. They were very hard working people, and amid a difficult situation, gave my sisters and me a decent life, despite our poverty. My parents never allowed for us to feel or believe we were entitled in any way. We were taught that you get an honest day's pay for an honest day's work.

In taking those two actions, it made a big difference in how I thought and deciding what goals I wanted to achieve for myself. Over time, one of those goals was wanting to become a Soldier and ultimately an Army officer. In the beginning, I believed that I was destined to be a professional football player, as did 99.9% of the boys who grew up in my environment. After failing out of college the first time, I was motivated to take a different path. The only conceivable option to developing a professional career was to enter the military. After failing out of college, I found a day labor job and even worked at a mental institution for a while. I recognized very quickly neither of these jobs were what I wanted in life. I initially tried to get into the Air Force. I failed to get into the Air Force twice, or rather didn't get a score on the Armed Services Vocational Aptitude Battery (ASVAB) high enough to get into the Air Force. The ASVAB is the skills qualification test in which the military uses to determine which jobs a new recruit has an aptitude for and will potentially be most successful in accomplishing. After those multiple failures, I went to work at a lumber yard until I got the courage to go back again to try to get into the military. This time I went to an Army recruiter. Yep, the first time I didn't make it. I failed once again. However, the second time I scored high enough to get into the Army.

One day while at basic training, our platoon was at the weapons qualification range. I was lying beside a guy who was a 2nd lieutenant. By that time through our classes and training, the Army had taught us the difference between being and enlisted Soldier and being a commissioned officer. In my estimation, being an officer definitely had more perks. As I laid there watching him, and, in particular, looking at that shiny "gold bar" on his patrol-cap, I began to wonder what it took to be an officer. He couldn't fire his weapon to save his life. He was missing targets left and right. I grew up hunting and fishing. That was how we survived and put food on the table. I was hitting all of my targets. I thought to myself, "If I can shoot better than this guy, then I too can be an officer." That moment began the long journey of becoming an Army officer. Over the course of almost six years, I had to take the ASVB almost ten times. This meant failure after failure after failure, until I finally exceeded the 110 point minimum score with a score of 112, which only granted me the "opportunity to apply" for Officer Candidate School (OCS). The score did not in any way permit me admittance into the course.

Over time I applied and was eventually admitted to the OCS. About seven weeks after my acceptance to Officer Candidate School, I was participating in our daily morning physical training. On this particular day, instead of participating in the standard Army calisthenics, we were allowed to play "combat soccer." *Hooah*! All was going well until, towards the end of the training, as luck would have it a Soldier stepped on my left foot. I immediately screamed out in pain. All I could think about was OCS. What now? I was rushed over to the troop medical clinic. Sitting there, worried beyond measure, I kept trying to convince myself that it was probably only a bad sprain. Oh, how wrong I was. When the x-rays came back, the doctor called me into his office and said, "Your ankle has been broken in three places." I withered in disbelief. Maybe the diagnosis was incorrect, or maybe the x-ray was inaccurate. An hour later, it was confirmed as I was having a cast placed on my left foot and leg all the way up to (but not past) my left knee.

I notified my higher headquarters, explained what had happened and asked for guidance. The guidance I was given was very simple, direct and to the point: reapply or report to class. I needed further clarification on what exactly "reapply" meant. I was thinking that maybe that meant I should reapply for another class date. No, it meant to reapply through the entire process which took almost six years the first time! I chose the latter option. After only a few weeks, I had my doctor remove the cast and I reported to Fort Benning, Georgia in the middle of the summer. I went through the entire OCS program with my left foot broken in three places, never once wanting to make a sick call.

F+RR=S

Failure + Right Response = Success

Chapter Fourteen

FAILURE CAN CAUSE A LIEUTENANT TO "DESPAIR"

"Failure is the inevitable cul de sac on the road to success."
-Peter Guber, Author & Businessman

As I rounded the corner of the Kenner Army Medical Facility in Fort Lee, Virginia, I saw one of our school's finest lieutenants coming towards me. He recognized me and greeted me with a half-smile. Instantly, I knew something was wrong. This is a young man who is always motivated and full of energy, his half-smile not matching his typical demeanor. I could see in his eyes the look of despair. Instead of being full of life and motivation, there was this look of utter loss and lack of hope. I thought he was going to cry. It almost broke my heart to see him like this. He seemed to have given up. I wondered what the cause of his hopelessness was. Had something horrible happened to a family member or someone close to him? Had a girlfriend broken up with him? Had he lost a best friend? Had he gotten an assignment for his first duty station that he wasn't excited about? Most of our lieutenants are very confident and they matriculate into the Army from civilian life very well. A lot of them believe with their whole hearts that they are ready to go, to fight and win our nation's wars (and most are correct, by the way).

I looked at this young man, completely stopped smiling and asked, "Lieutenant, what's wrong? Is everything all right?" He dropped his head to stare at the waxed and polished floor and said, "Sir, I've been recycled," Recycling, or being held over to repeat a certain phase of a course while in training, is by far the most feared reprimanding in military training on all levels. Recycling generally means having to go back through the entire training--regardless of where you are in the program--which means you must spend additional time trying to get up to speed, learning and understanding the information, and meeting the requirements to be able to graduate.

The Quartermaster Basic Officer Leaders Course (QM BOLC) is designed to train lieutenants with the skills needed to overcome challenges and succeed in their first unit of assignment by creating, maintaining and cultivating an ethically sound learning environment that fosters the development of leadership, problem solving, and technical skills. The QM BOLC is approximately 16 weeks long and divided into the areas of Professional Development, Common Core, Tactics, Common Logistics, Aerial Delivery and Field Services Department (ADFSD), tactical logistics (TACLOG), Global Combat Support System - Army (GCSS-A), Automated Logistics, Subsistence, Petroleum and Water Operations (PWO), Training Management, Property Accountability, and Mortuary Affairs.[10]

---

[10] https://alu.army.mil/officers/bold/quartermaster.html

He was in his 13th week when he was recycled; Three weeks from graduating and had to start fresh. Before I could even ask, he started explaining that it was his academic performance which caused him to "fail" (this was his exact wording, by the way). He was not able to comprehend all of the training and information that was being taught to the class. As I looked at him with despair in his heart and heavy thoughts on his mind, I said, "LT, head up." I asked him if I could share a story with him. He agreed to allow me to share and began listening intently.

The first thing I shared with him was this: "Failure is not the problem, what you do with this failure is." I began sharing with him a story about when I was a student at the Infantry Officer Candidate School (OCS) at Fort Benning many years ago. I, too, had a single failure which transformed how I look at that failure. I shared with him how at OCS you are tested emotionally, physically, spiritually, and of course academically. In fact, at OCS, some of the instructors only wanted what they considered *the best of the best* to graduate and didn't necessarily care if anyone graduated at all. That's not how all of the instructors felt, but that was the spirit of the course and still is to this day. I agree with this concept. After all, as it is with all commissioning sources, graduates of the Officer Candidate School would more than likely at some point be leading America's treasure into combat.

I told him that my single failure came from the Field Artillery exam. It was heavy in math and long on equations, a subject I knew very little about. As he continued to listen, there was a small glimmer in his eyes. I said that during this entire course (which was 14 weeks long), any student could fail only one exam on any subject matter. During which time, we would receive only one retest. If a student failed the retest, the cadre had the option of recycling the candidate or completely dropping them from the entire course.

I shared with LT that was the first and only exam I failed while I attended OCS. I explained to him how I refocused. I didn't get down on myself. Yes, I was disappointed and had despair, but I never quit; I never gave up; I never accepted defeat. I was given a second chance. I went on to mention a laundry list of my academic failures. He responded with astonishment, saying, "WOW, I never would have thought that." I nodded my head in agreement and said, "You don't get to become a Colonel in the Army without failing at some point in your career." I quickly mentioned some of my accomplishments also, with a smile. We don't want lieutenants thinking poorly of colonels, right? He almost smiled.

At the end of our conversation, I reinforced the fact that this singular failure is not the problem, it's the beginning of your success if you respond to it correctly. I said to him, "As was given to me, it has also been offered up to you--a second chance." By now his huge smile had returned, the life had come back into his eyes, and looking at me, he said, "I got this Sir." To which I responded, "*Hooah!*"

As I watched him disappear down the corridors of that clinic with some more pep in his step and glide in his stride, he gently slapped the wall as if to say, "I'm going to do this," and I knew at that point that he understood. I walked away fully confident that this young Army officer was going to be successful and graduate in 16 weeks and lastly, as I walked out the doors of the clinic, I thanked God for this opportunity once again to remember that I failed so others may be successful.

Chapter Fifteen

THERE IS VALUE IN YOUR FAILURE

"The reason people don't value you, is because you don't value yourself."
-Anonymous

Beliefs are theories that we make about our existence, our experiences, and humanity, which our values tend to follow. Values are those standards that we deem important. If we aren't careful, our beliefs can completely control every decision we make, particularly regarding failure. Generally, we are taught to believe that failure has no value at all. If there is any value that can be found in failure, it's normally in the form of a negative reference. When we are conflicted with what we were taught versus what we honestly believe, it can create an internal struggle in our ability to challenge ourselves. In order to gain clarity and understand that failure is valuable, it's a good idea to question if there is any merit in failing.

In order to challenge your values and beliefs you must know who you are. When I was growing up, I always had this inner confusion as to who I was. It stemmed from not understanding why my sisters had somewhat different beliefs and values that I had. Although we grew up in the same household and were taught the same rules, I always thought and believed differently than they did. As best as I could tell, it had very little to do with the difference in our genders. Even though I knew I thought differently, which was demonstrated simply by conversations we would have, I still adopted some of their same values and beliefs. It was the same regarding the community and the neighborhood I grew up in. I could see, based upon decisions I was making, that my innermost spirit was struggling.

My personal values and beliefs didn't match up with who I was at my core. Regarding education, failure was not accepted very well. At all cost, passing to the next grade was paramount in my family and in the community in which I was reared. Why? Because failure or passing to the next grade was a reflection upon our families. One position was rejected, and the other was expected. With failure, you could expect dejection while with passing to the next grade, succession. In our small rural community, there were two major events every school year. One was report card day, the other was the end of the school year. This would be the time to see who was getting the best grades and which children would be passing on to the next grade level, and who would remain (or be "retained" as we affectionately referred to it) in the same grade level in the next school year. Success was defined as being promoted and moving on to the next grade level, not necessarily *learning* as a concept. The values and beliefs about failure in general and failure for me personally changed drastically after I left home and ventured into the world.

I changed my attitude on the subject of failure and thought of it as an event whereby I could learn, rather than understanding it as shame, guilt, and the end of something never to be gained.

Following are some things I learned about the value of failure throughout my life and my educational experiences.

SOME VALUES OF FAILURE:
Teaches humility
Gives Strength to be courageous
Offers the ability to find a better way
Reveal our weaknesses which allows us to get better
Allows us to see value in all things
Demonstrates that no one is always right
Teaches strength of character
Allows for growth
Encourages multiple experiences
Motivates us to be the person we are meant to be

Chapter Sixteen

WHEN FAILURE MAKES YOU FEEL INADEQUATE AND PEOPLE CALL YOU STUPID, NEVER GIVE UP-- EVEN WHEN YOU FAIL REPEATEDLY

"You don't get what you wish for, you don't get what you hope for, you get what you believe."

-Oprah Winfrey

I transcribed a discussion that Chinese businessman Jack Ma was having on the "Motivation Madness" YouTube channel. In one segment, Ma described some factors in his life which he found to be important. For one, he did not have a rich father. He had applied three times for university, each time getting rejected! He applied for Harvard ten times--all failed attempts! They didn't even want to see him, he said. He wanted to try one more time to apply for school, so he went to the local teacher's college, which was considered third or fourth class in his city. He ultimately landed a job, but he mentioned how difficult it was for him and how he was so frustrated--he was teaching at the university and his pay was only ten dollars a month. Because he could not find a good job in 1994, he decided he was going to use something called the Internet as a way for him to create his own business. There were friends in his circle who ridiculed him and told him his idea was stupid, echoing that they had never heard about the Internet and that he knew nothing about computers.

Mr. Ma said that he never thought that he was smart. No one ever believed that he could be successful because he thought differently. For three months, he tried to borrow nearly $3000.00 from banks, but was turned away. He and his team talked to between thirty and forty venture capitalists about his business idea. They all told him to forget it. Many said the name of the company, Alibaba, was terrible. Mr. Ma said that he believed strongly in this company he was trying to create, and believed that it could be big. Although he thought it could be big, he said he never thought it could be as big as it has grown to be. The Alibaba team were eventually able to acquire $50,000 from eighteen individual investors. For the first three years, the company didn't even accumulate $1.00 in revenue from their business. Over time, customers began to say that Ma's business was helping them, and little by little as the business began to grow. As of 2018, Alibaba has amassed a fortune of over $500 billion. After a success this large, people were now telling Mr. Ma that he was so smart, and asking how he got the idea to make such a company like this.

Failure was never the problem for Jack Ma. Persistence in the face of failure has been the magic formula for the formation of Alibaba as a company. Mr. Ma wasn't granted three wishes-- what he didn't do was complain and blame others.

What he *did* do was never give up on what he believed in, even after repeated failures. Always remember to hold on, because on the other side of your failures is something good!

Chapter Seventeen

FAILURE AND SUCCESS ARE TWO SIDES OF THE SAME COIN

"If you try to fail, and succeed, which have you done?"
-George Carlin, stand-up comedian

One of the biggest obstacles in the way of seeing failure as a positive is the inability to change your perspective and your mindset. The term "dialectical" deals with open-minded thinking. Dialectical thinking refers to the ability to view issues from multiple perspectives and to arrive at the most sensible and reasonable understanding of seemingly contradictory information and positions.

Zeno of Elea

Two commanders were arguing over this photo. One saw an old lady, while the other saw and beautiful young woman. Neither wanted to give way and see it from the other's perspective. If only they could have viewed it from a dialectical standpoint, they would have seen that they were both right. For one to see, understand and embrace failure as success, the dialectical way of thinking and mindset is a *must*, especially for the readers of this book.

There is always more than one way to see a situation and there can always be more than one opinion, idea, dream, thought or way to get to the truth. If we retrain ourselves and change the way we experience, embrace and understand failure from a negative expectation to a positive revelation, we can literally transform this world for the better.

Chapter Eighteen

WHEN YOU FAIL, EMBRACE IT

"People fail not because they can, but because they believe they can."
-George A. Milton

If you embrace failure, what's the worst thing that could happen? Instead of worrying about the outcome, embrace your failures with strength and confidence. Everyone has failed in the past, is currently falling into failure, and will fail in the future. We all fail from time to time. Everyone makes mistakes. React to your failure and mistakes positively instead of responding negatively. It's your choice. When you fail, don't think of yourself as a "failure," or a "mistake," or as someone who has no value. *Of course* you have value.

When you fail or make a mistake, do not begin believing that you are not worthy of a fantastic, eventful, wonderful life. Never say to yourself that you are worthless, no matter how many times you've been told that by others. Move your thinking and your mind away from this sort of nonsense. If you think a certain way long enough, eventually you will believe it. Therefore, commit to developing your thinking to accepting failure as just another event. Own the failure and the mistakes. Try not to repeat them again, but stop with the self-hatred, negative talk and wallowing in self-pity. Focus on the positive aspects of failure, such as the lessons you can gain from failure, and the fact that you can get a second (and sometimes a third) chance to get it right. Focus on the fact that your failure may simply mean that you need to change direction in your life. Or, maybe you need to change the people with whom you've been hanging around. You have the power to delete them from your life or to remove yourself from theirs.

If you develop the mindset that there aren't positive lessons to be gained from failure and making mistakes, or that there aren't any benefits to failure, then you just aren't trying hard enough to change your perspective. Maybe you have gotten comfortable with fearing failure and allowing failure to control your life. If you are going to have the discipline and wherewithal to change your outcome and outlook on how you embrace failure, it will first start with how you think. "As a man thinketh in his heart, so is he!" (Proverbs 23:7) Your thinking becomes a belief, which turns into a value, which eventually results in an action. Whether it's positive or negative, the choice is yours.

Neuroscientists are finding that we spend our entire lives being conditioned. If we can condition ourselves to think about failure in a negative sense, we can also learn how to condition our minds (and eventually our actions) to turn failure into positive energy and responses. Through a lifetime of events, our brains have learned what to expect, whether it happens that way or not. Because our brains expect it, we often achieve exactly what we're thinking whether we intend to or not. Some people are referring to this as the Law of Attraction or the universe delivering what we spend most of our thoughts on. Replace negative thoughts of failure with positive thoughts of benefits from failing, such as lessons learned, more opportunity, change of direction in life, change of career, change of relationship, change of expectations. Change, if done correctly, is good.

Chapter Nineteen

MY FAILURE TO BECOME A CHAPLAIN

"In the midst of chaos, there is also opportunity."

-Sun-Tzu

When I arrived at Southwestern Baptist Theological Seminary in Fort Worth, Texas, I had recently experienced massive failure. I was facing family issues, career change, no place to live, no support system, and no job. None of that mattered, because I was going to a place that I had thought at that time was the holiest place on the planet. Although my experience there is one of my most cherished, it was far from perfect. There were many challenges there, just like there were (and still are) throughout the rest of my life.

There were many amazing professors, instructors, administration and staff members, and the student body (for the most part) were some of the most sincere people I have ever met. I have lots of fond memories from my time at Southwestern. Interestingly, the vast majority of students I interacted with came there with similar reasons to mine regarding why they wanted to be a chaplain in the Army. They wanted to serve their country, they wanted to make the world a better place, and they wanted to join the Chaplaincy Corps and serve in the military in the aftermath of September 11th. Some came from a long line of ministers, and it was in keeping with family tradition to continue that legacy. Many were looking for significance in their lives. As we often espouse in church talk, I believed I was called to Southern Baptist Theological Seminary (SWBTS) to go into ministry and to be an educator in the church, as well as a college professor (I accomplished all those goals without being a chaplain).

As I mentioned earlier, along with this amazing experience, I did have a few challenges. One such challenge was in my efforts to become a chaplain. Although I had a military background in the Army, I had never really considered becoming a chaplain because I never felt worthy enough to serve in ministry at that level. At least, not until I joined an Army Reserve unit in Grand Prairie, Texas. I had yearned for and was missing being in the Army after I had gotten off active duty and went back to school, so after entering SWBTS, I eventually joined the Army Reserves. At one of our battle assemblies (or drill weekends, as they were known when I had first joined the Army), I was talking to our battalion chaplain. I listened to what he was sharing with me in reference to his responsibilities to our Soldiers, which piqued my interest. Yep, as all good committed Christians do, I sought God's guidance in prayer. After praying for his direction and guidance and talking to my family for many months, it was my belief that I was "being called" to be a chaplain in the Army. I reached out to the Army Chaplain Corps. To my surprise, it was relatively easy to find key personnel to point me in the right direction to get the ball rolling. There were many hurdles I had to jump over, but none were insurmountable--except for one.

The key for me becoming a Chaplain was to obtain a letter of endorsement from my denomination. This is not only specific to the denomination I belonged to, it was (and remains to this day for the most part) Army/Military policy. By the time I was called to be a Chaplain, I already completed all requirements and had graduated with my first Master's degree in Religious Education from SWBTS, and had even started classes in a doctoral program at SWBTS. Yep, I was enrolled and working on my Doctor of Ministry degree, so I figured I was good to go! Well, not exactly. Remember that letter of endorsement I had mentioned earlier? That was a solid requirement for the Army from my denomination.

After receiving this guidance from the Army, I set up several appointments with faculty and staff members at Southwestern. As I inquired as how to best obtain the much-needed endorsement, it became very clear that I would need a Master of Divinity degree. They were all very supportive, but all very clear that there would be absolutely no negotiations on accepting my Master's in Religious Education for a substitute for the Master of Divinity degree.

My last chance was to get an appointment with the resident Army Chaplain/ professor on campus who happened to be a one-star General Officer (Brigadier General). I couldn't believe my "luck." I would appeal to his sensibilities of being a Soldier and my status of already having completed a master's degree, as well as the Army's willingness to accept me and bring me on active duty as a Chaplain, as long as I had the support of my denomination. As I walked into his immaculate office, it became very clear by the photos and awards on his wall that he had served many years as a pastor in the civilian world, as well as a chaplain in the Army. I jumped right into why I was there. He was very professional, but matter-of-factually said that in order to gain an endorsement, I would need to gain acceptance into the Master of Divinity degree program and complete that field of study.

I wanted to make sure I was clear on what I was hearing from him and that he was clear about the fact that I was already working on my Doctor of Ministry degree at SWBTS already. So, I asked in order for me to gain the much-needed endorsement, if I would either need to complete *both* my Doctor of Ministry *and* the Masters of Divinity degree simultaneously, or drop out of the Doctor of Ministry program and focus on the Masters of Divinity degree. He verified that that was correct. After much prayer, I asked myself what the real reason for attending the seminary in the first place. The top three were being in service to God, serving people, and my goal of becoming a Christian educator at a university. After talking to personnel at the Army Chaplaincy program, it was clear that I was going to fail and not be able to gain a Chaplaincy commission. I would fail to gain the full support of the General, the faculty and staff in accepting my progress towards my Doctor of Ministry or my Masters in Religion Education from Southwestern to gain support in becoming a chaplain.

I decided (after 17 hours towards the Doctor of Ministry) to drop out of the program and try a different route. By the way, I had all A's in the program, so this time it wasn't because of my failing grades! A few years after dropping out of Southwestern Baptist Theological Seminary, I went on to become the Education Minister at an intercity city church in a small Texas city, and eventually the Army offered me an active duty job as a university professor. *Hooah*! All this is to say that failing to become an Army chaplain didn't stop me from accomplishing many of my goals in life. In fact, *because* I failed at becoming an Army Chaplain, my Army Career took me in a totally different direction than I had expected, and I was able to accomplish so much more.

Some of my crowning accomplishments have been becoming a University Professor, commanding in combat, briefing ambassadors, briefing foreign governments, earning another Master's degree from the United States Army War College, meeting the Secretary of Defense, working with multiple foreign governments, and eventually becoming an Officer Candidate School Hall of Fame Soldier. This is just to name a few. Failure was not the problem, it was the beginning of my success. My response was to find another way to serve.

$$F+RR=S$$

Failure + Right Response = Success

Chapter Twenty

FROM ORDINARY TO EXTRAORDINARY

"Do not let what you cannot do interfere with what you can do."
-John Wooden, American Basketball Coach

God uses ordinary people to accomplish extraordinary events. I was watching a documentary of the 2019 National Collegiate Athletic Association (NCAA) that focused on Coach Jimmy Valvano, (or "Jimmy V," as he was affectionately known). The former basketball player, broadcaster and coach of North Carolina State University mentioned that when he was 16 years of age, he was listening to a well-respected leader in his community. Jimmy explained that at that point in his life, he desperately wanted and needed direction and guidance for his existence. He went on to explain that as he sat in the audience, hoping to hear something amazing and motivational. He expected that he would hear something that would give him purpose. As the speaker was well into his speech, Jimmy was listening intently for a sign. The speaker simply said, "just like most of us in this room, most of the people that God has created, are just ordinary people." Jimmy said he remembered thinking, "Huh? That's it?" and, after a pause, the speaker said, "and from those ordinary people God accomplishes extraordinary things!"

Those were the words Jimmy needed to hear. He said that that one statement on that day put him on the path of becoming the accomplished coach that he was destined to be and accomplishing greatness, specifically taking North Carolina State University in 1983 to a national basketball championship and winning the national title. This goes to show that no matter what, you can never allow your fear of failure to hold you back. Allow yourself to be useful as a vessel to accomplish extraordinary things. Whomever your God is, wherever you transcend to after you leave this earth, prior to leaving, allow your God to use your talents, gifts and abilities to accomplish extraordinary events. In the process you will fail, but remember that failure is not the problem--when it happens, push through and learn from it, and remind yourself that you were born to accomplish extraordinary events. Always remember to hold on, because on the other side of your failures is something good!

Although winning the national championship didn't happen overnight, coach Jimmy V set goals for the next opportunity. When you fail, set goals so that the next time it happens, you will at least have some successes to compare the failures to. North Carolina State never gave up on their dreams of winning a National Championship, and eventually they did win with a great leader at the helm.

Chapter Twenty-One

THE CHAPLAIN ASSISTANT'S FAILURE

"Bravery is the capacity to perform properly even when scared half to death."
                                    -General Omar N. Bradley

When I think about failure, one of my most standout moments was when I was in my third of five total deployments. I was commanding a unit in Mosul, Iraq. The battalion chaplain was someone whom I had become fond of. It wasn't that way initially, though. When the chaplain and I first met, he was on a mission to inform me that not only were my Soldiers not happy, but since he was now caught in my crosshairs, nor was he going to be happy. There weren't any prayers during this conversation--well, at least none that were spoken aloud. Who knows, maybe he said a quiet one or two.

About two weeks into our deployment, the chaplain (or "Chappy," as I called him) needed a lift to another Forward Operating Base (FOB). In a staff meeting, my boss asked who was willing to give the chaplain a ride to one of the other bases. I immediately raised my hand to make sure everyone in the room knew that I wanted that mission. As I raised my hand, I flashed a big ol' grin and looked directly at Chappy. He looked at me and tried to smile, but could only muster a faint grin. If looks were words, I could tell he was profaning me up and down that meeting area. As luck would have it, I got called away to go on another mission, but my unit was still responsible for the mission of escorting the chaplain to the other FOB. I relinquished my vehicle to Chappy and pulled the team together that was accountable for getting him to the other side. I made it very clear that our chaplain had an incredibly important mission, and it was their duty to ensure he arrived safely. Not long after the vehicles roared down the dusty main road of the FOB and out the back gates, the convoy came under attack. The convoy eventually made it safely to the other FOB.

The chaplain was a little shaken up, and that one ride totally changed our relationship. From that day forward, Chappy understood firsthand why I was interested in leading my Soldiers and not interested in being their friend. Upon his arrival back at our FOB the next day, he said to me, "Sir, I now understand why you lead the way you do; It's war, and it's dangerous, and your mission is to ensure as best you can all of your Soldiers make it back to their families." I nodded very slowly and said, "Chappy, it's about *leadership*, not *liker-ship!*"

Not long after my conversation with Chappy, my driver came running up to me and asked if I had heard about the chaplain's assistant. I hadn't, and asked if he was ok. What happened? I knew the chaplain's assistant reasonably well, because anytime I was conversing with Chappy, his assistant was close by, and for good reason. In war, chaplains are by regulation not allowed to carry a weapon, at least not legally! The chaplain's assistant has many duties, and sometimes can better relate to the Soldiers since they are enlisted members, also. The chaplain assistant's most important mission is protecting the chaplain. In other words, he is a bodyguard sworn to carry a weapon and protect the chaplain. My driver explained to me that after the convoy had come under attack the previous evening and then came to safety, the chaplain's assistant had decided that he no longer wanted to carry his weapon, and wasn't going to ever pick it back up. Technically, Soldiers who can't carry a weapon aren't allowed to be in combat. This was a problem if proven to be true. Not to mention, I kind of liked the chaplain now.

Prior to this incident outside the wire, I had numerous conversations with the chaplain's assistant, and explained that it was very important that he protect the chaplain. On each occasion, he assured me that no matter what happened, he would be ready. He had me convinced, that's for sure. So, I was very surprised and didn't want to believe what I was hearing. I had to hear this from the chaplain's assistant himself if I was going to believe that this was true. After searching multiple areas, I finally saw him. As he approached me, I did indeed notice he wasn't carrying his weapon. After a courteous greeting, I inquired as to where his weapon was. He said, without blinking an eye, "I put my weapon down." After hearing that statement, I don't know if it was the beads of sweat that were now dripping off my face, my silence as I stared at him, or the wrinkles on my forehead, which indicated to him that I wasn't very happy to hear that. I thought for a moment, and after I regained my composure I simply asked him why. His answer was classic--This Soldier who--had taken an oath to not only protect and defend our constitution, but had also sworn to protect the chaplain--said this: "God told me to put my weapon down." I wanted to say, "What the hell?" but instead I burst into laughter, which I couldn't help. *What God?*

Yep, sure enough, he was talking about Jehovah. He went into this exhausting diatribe about how he had chosen the wrong military occupational specialty (MOS), and at one point said that he would give the bonus money he received back to the Army. I said, "Son, we don't want the money back. What you need to do is protect the chaplain." He was adamant that he could not do so because God had told him to lay the weapon down. I got very quiet, and I began to look skyward. I raised my right hand to my right ear to demonstrate that I was listening and wanted to make sure I was hearing correctly. As I held my hand to my ear, I said, "Yes, I understand." I dropped my hand, looked at the chaplain's assistant and said, "Soldier, God just told me to tell you to pick up your weapon and go protect the chaplain." His reply was, "I don't believe that," and I immediately said, "nor do I believe He told you to put your weapon down."

I brought this matter up to my commander, and unfortunately my boss never made the Soldier pick up his weapon. He reassigned the Soldier to menial duties and requisitioned another chaplain's assistant. From that day forward, that Soldier was not able to walk anywhere on the FOB with his head held proudly, although he was allowed to remain in the combat zone until the end of his deployment. This was a terrible failure, in my opinion. This single event, throughout the remainder of my military career, made me wonder, "Does war cause cowardice, or reveal cowardice?" I am of the opinion that war reveals something that was already there.

After our deployment, I don't know what happened to that Soldier, nor do I know what he is currently doing in his life--but I hope that he learned a valuable lesson regarding his experience in Mosul, Iraq, and I genuinely hope it was a positive lesson that he gained. Failure to protect the chaplain wasn't the only problem. Had he assumed the duties he had been sworn to, the chaplain's assistant could have used that experience to learn many lessons such as integrity, character, keeping his agreements, and, most importantly, that *it was never about him*. If the chaplain's assistant should ever read this book, he will have to be the one who decides what, if anything of value, was learned from that experience.

Chapter Twenty-Two

DO NOT PUNISH YOURSELF WHEN YOU FAIL

"Failure is part of the human condition, there is no escaping it!"
    -Unknown

Way too many people blame not only others, but also themselves, when they fail. I am reminded of a story I read that illustrates why punishment probably isn't a good idea: There were these two brothers who were at a BBQ-party. A friend of theirs approached them, and after initiating pleasantries asked, "How's that new bird dog?" The younger brother looked at his older brother, then looked back at their friend and said, "It ain't going too good. That is one of the most un-trainable hunting dogs we have ever owned." The older brother said, "I don't think it's the dog at all. I think it's this new technique you are using." The friend looks at the younger brother and asks, "What does he mean, what new technique are you using?" The younger brother looks at the friend and says, "Well I paid this guy $1,000.00, and it just *ain't working*." The friend says, "Explain exactly what you're doing."

The younger brother says, "I have been trying to train that dog to not crap on the floor. The dog craps on the floor, I grab him, shoved his nose in the crap, pound him on the ass with a newspaper, and then throw him out the kitchen window into the backyard." The friend asks, "So what exactly is the problem again?" The younger brother says, "Now the dog takes a crap on the floor and jumps out the kitchen window!"

This was probably not the "response" the younger brother was aiming for.

Chapter Twenty-Three

GET COMFORTABLE WITH BEING UNCOMFORTABLE

"Failure is a feeling long before it becomes an actual result. It's vulnerability that breeds with self-doubt and then is escalated, often deliberately, by fear."
-Michelle Obama, Former First Lady of the United States

Why are most people more comfortable with talking about success rather than failure? In a single word: stigma. Yes, many believe failure represents something that is tainted, contaminated, polluted, stained, shameful, disgraceful and somehow not worthy of praise. From a very early age, children are taught that only success is acceptable. Unfortunately, and too often, lots of people take to heart this message and failure becomes an albatross around the necks of millions of people as they maneuver through the maze of life, never being able to forget that if they don't win, they are not good enough. After all, no one loves a loser, right? And if you want love and attention, you must win and never lose. Of course, we love our kids, whether or not they become as successful as we would like them to be. However, sometimes, if we aren't careful, we can send the wrong messages to our children and give them the impression that success at any cost is standard, and failure (for any reason) is unacceptable.

For example, look at "Operation Varsity Blues," the 2019 college admissions bribery scandal that is supposedly the largest in United States' history. Caught up in this scam were several people that included some of Hollywood's elite and their families. There are a few lessons to be learned from this outrage. First, failure is not remotely tolerable. Had failure been bearable or acceptable, perhaps there would not have been the need to "stack the deck" in hopes of guaranteeing acceptance in some of the most prestigious universities and colleges in the United States. Second, success (even if it costs millions of dollars and disgraces their families) is worth it. Third, the fact that your family is well-connected and is stacked with privilege means that you're entitled, and that you don't have to work for what you get. All that matters is that you get in and get a leg up, become successful, and not fail. Fourth (and the saddest testament), these parents did not believe in their kids.

What an awful lesson the parents were teaching their children about failure and success. There are many reasons why anyone might behave in a similar way as these families did, but I am convinced that one of those reasons is because the parents were not ok with their kids failing. They wanted to guarantee their offspring something that life itself doesn't guarantee: success. Conversely, life does guarantee that we will all fail. Does failure really imply a lack of success?

I think not. It is my opinion that failure is the beginning of your success, as I have stated many times throughout this book. The issue is not failure, but how we *perceive* what failure *represents*. Ask anyone if they'd prefer to succeed or fail, and they will look at you like you're crazy. You will get a "deer staring into headlights" response. Often you will see this look of, "Are you stupid?" Of course, we all want to win, right? Why is that the case? One answer is because we have learned to place a higher value on winning over failing.

Chapter Twenty-Four

CHANGE HOW YOU RESPOND TO FAILURE

"The past cannot be changed. The future is yet in your power."
-Unknown

The power to change is in your hands. You must have the desire and the drive to do so. Change is not something that always comes easy, but nor is it impossible to achieve. If change is to occur, then there must first be the will to change. If there is a will, then there is the potential for change. If you are able to change but are simply unwilling, then the outcome of change will probably be unsuccessful.

WHO ARE YOU? DO YOU EVEN KNOW?

*"I am not what I think I am, I am not what you think I am.
I am what I think you think I am."*
-Charles Horton Cooley

Why do we try to become who others think we should be? Why do we worry so much about what people think about us? In his book, *"The Success Principles:*

How to Get from Where You Are to Where You Want to Be," Jack Canfield chronicles Dr. Daniel Amen's **18/40/60** Rule:

When you're 18, you worry about what everybody is thinking of you; When you're 40, you don't give a darn what anybody thinks of you; When you're 60, you realize nobody's been thinking about you at all.[11]

When anyone calls you a failure, don't ever accept that as a label. Consider it a badge of honor knowing that this is simply an experience which will give you an opportunity to perhaps change. Although you should not be overly concerned about being called a failure, you should also not *think of yourself* as a failure, because you aren't. You may just need to change the direction of your life, or maybe the way you think about failure in the first place. If people think you are a failure, that's their problem. Don't make it your problem.

If you could have a conversation with your younger self regarding failure, what advice would you give to your younger self? How would you advise your younger self to respond to failure when it happens? How could you explain to your younger self which path you should take when it comes to understanding failure? How could you teach your younger self to embrace and accept failure? How could you demonstrate to your younger self that failure is just an

---

[11] Jack Canfield and Janet Switzer, The Success Principles, How to Get from Where you Are to Where You Want to Be. (195 Broadway, New Your, NY 10007, Harper Collins, 2005, 2015), page 58.

experience or a journey, and not a destination? How could you train your younger self to see failure as a positive and not something negative, and therefore to be feared? In order for you to embrace failure as something positive and replace those negative thoughts, there has to be a certain amount of change involved, whether it be a change of thoughts, ideas, beliefs, values, or a change in your actions. There are potentially many paths to and phases of change. Below is what I have been taught throughout my years as a professional Soldier with the responsibilities of training and counseling Soldiers.

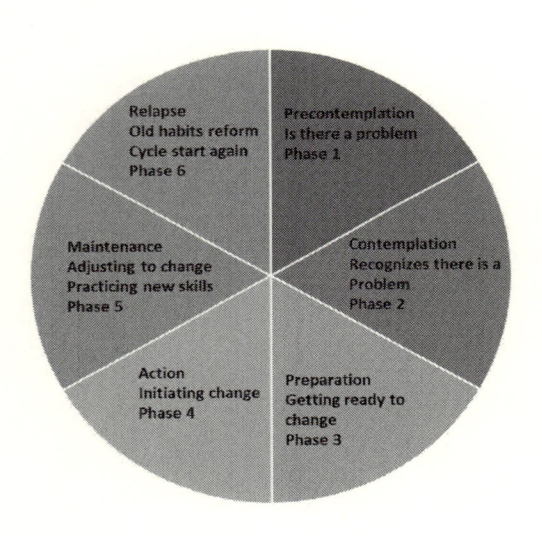

Phases of Change

- **Phase 1 – Precontemplation:** Is there a problem
- **Phase 2 – Contemplation:** Recognizes there is a problem
- **Phase 3 – Preparation:** Getting ready to change
- **Phase 4 – Action:** Initiating change
- **Phase 5 – Maintenance:** Adjusting to change, Practicing new skills
- **Phase 6 – Relapse:** Old habits reform, Cycle start again

One of the critical assets of being a Soldier has always been to remain flexible. Why? Because there is always going to be change. Change is good! *Change your experience with failure*. Where are you in this process changing, how you see and relate to failure? List where you are. List where you want to be:

PRE-CONTEMPLATION_____

CONTEMPLATION_____

PREPARATION_____

ACTION_____

MAINTENANCE_____

RELAPSE_____

INVICTUS

Out of the night that covers me,
Black as the pit from pole to pole,
I thank whatever gods may be
For my unconquerable soul.

In the fell clutch of circumstance
I have not winced nor cried aloud.
Under the bludgeonings of chance
My head is bloody, but unbowed.

Beyond this place of wrath and tears
Looms but the Horror of the shade,
And yet the menace of the years
Finds and shall find me unafraid.

It matters not how strait the gate,
How charged with punishments the scroll,
I Am The Master Of My Fate,
I Am The Captain Of My Soul.

~ William Ernest Henley

---

12   https://www.google.com/search?q=william+ernest+henley+invictus&biw=1034&bih=620&tbm=isch&source=iu&ictx=1&fir=wEJNMHloy5M-iM%253A%252CYvLYeAdqobgdWM%252C%252Fm%252F03rpy&vet=1&usg=AI4_-kQlteUaXwp0Wo9qxueEXrHqZ0K2mQ&sa=X&ved=2ahUKEwjuhs6a0tXlAhVyUN8KHSCWA5gQ_B0wG3oECAgQAw#imgrc=wEJNMHloy5M-iM:

Chapter Twenty-Five

YOUR THOUGHTS ARE CONTRIBUTING TO YOUR FAILURE

"He or she who believes they are a failure, or not, is correct!"
-George A. Milton

If you keep on thinking that you're a failure, you will continue responding in ways that you and everyone else will expect for failures to respond. Your thoughts become your actions. As it is thought, so let it be done. Every action or decision we make starts with a thought, which eventually results in a maneuver of some sort. In the Army, a maneuver is a large-scale exercise of troops, warships, and other forces; a carefully planned scheme or action, especially one involving deception; a movement or series of moves requiring skill and care. Our thoughts drive everything we do and everything we are and everything we will ever become, whether that be good or bad, positive or negative. If that's true, then it's critical how you think about failure.

You have the options of looking at failure from a positive perspective: Learning, growing, and developing an optimistic outlook on life. You can choose to create constructive, teachable moments in your life, or destructive, negative ones where you're always blaming others for your inadequate behavior combined with fear, paralysis, stigma, unwillingness to learn, stagnating, developing a poor outlook on life.

Chapter Twenty-Six
<u>DON'T TAKE OR MAKE FAILURE PERSONAL</u>

"I don't believe in failure. I believe that whatever you are to do if you do it to the best of your ability, there are lessons and nuggets in there that are success. I don't believe in failure, everything is used."

-Tyler Perry

Throughout my career, there were countless times when those who worked for me tried to make their personal and professional failures my responsibility. I was never one to blame others for my failures. This goes back to my rearing and the example I saw in my parents. Education wasn't their main focus; however, work definitely was. I don't want to give the impression that my parents didn't believe in my sisters and me being educated. They saw the value in a "good education," but neither of them graduated from high school, so their experiences and examples were more in line with receiving an honest day's pay for an honest day's work. My sisters and I were never allowed to play the blame game.

When I entered the workforce, I took the mentality of working hard and accepting my failures as my own. There were many times I failed in civilian life and as a Soldier, but blaming my supervisors wasn't the route I took. Sure, I was disappointed when something didn't work out for me, but instead of pointing my finger and accusing others, I went to my superiors and asked what I had done wrong and how to improve it. Surely, not everyone I worked for was always as eager to share with me how to get better, but there were some who did explain to me how to get better. In both examples, the responsibility for my failures and how to make it better was on *me* to get up to speed.

I was always sensitive to others who worked for me and how they responded to failure. I didn't allow for them to use failure as a crutch, but I was always willing to work with anyone who put in the work. When I failed at my job, I tried to remember not to take it personally. When others failed me, I didn't make their professional failure *my* problem. Instead, I did what the Army instilled in me: retraining (as long as the Soldier was willing to be retrained).

How does that joke about the psychologist go? "How many psychologists does it take to change a lightbulb? One, but the lightbulb must be willing to change!" I always lived by that principle. I still do!

<u>Listed are 12 steps to change your mindset regarding failure from Negative to Positive:</u>

1. Believe that it's possible to change your thoughts in the first place.
   If the mind can conceive it, you can achieve it.

2. Know yourself.
Too often we live our lives for others, not truly understanding who we are.

3. Accept yourself.
So much of our time is spent on berating and beating ourselves up.

4. Trust yourself.
To thine own self be true. You must be honest with yourself.

5. You must challenge yourself to see failure as positive.
To change, you must want to do something differently or think differently.

6. Change your attitude.
Your attitude will determine your altitude.

7. Retrain your mind, brain, thoughts, and actions to believe that failure has value.
Generally, we are taught that anything having to do with failure is futile.

8. You must visualize your failures as positive rather than as negative.
Seeing is believing.

9. You must make a decision to change your mindset.
You can choose how you respond to failure. **F+RR=S (Failure +Right Response = Success).**

10. You must take action on changing your thoughts and mindset.
It's not automatic, but with commitment and persistence it will become much easier.

11. You have to practice, practice, practice until your thoughts become positive.
Practice is where all championships are won.

12. You must "fully" embrace failure as a natural part of your life.
Failure is like taking a "full" breath, without it, can you truly live?

Chapter Twenty-Seven

IT BREAKS A MOTHER'S HEART TO SEE HER CHILD FAIL

"Life is really simple, but we insist on making it complicated."

-Confucius

What's a single father to do when for the *thousandth time* his child announces on a Saturday morning at 0300 (that's 3:00AM in civilian time), that she has lost her dental retainers, again? There are a multitude of choices one can make. One, look at the child and say something like, "What? Not again. Or you can say, "I am not going to pay anymore money for another retainer; it's your responsibility and you will have to figure out how to pay for it." Or, you can tear up the house looking for the retainer as though your life depends on it-- looking in the trash cans, underneath the beds, in closets, in the car, the bathroom, her bedroom, my bedroom (why would it be in my bedroom? Who knows?), or you can simply agree to pay the money to replace it. Of course, I chose to pay to replace the retainers. After all, what parent wants his daughter walking around with wonky teeth looking like Austin Powers? So yes, once again, I broke down and decided to pay.

That following Monday morning I found myself at my daughter's orthodontist's office. The last time we had seen her was about six months prior. I must admit, it was good to see the good doctor. Anytime we spoke it was always pleasant, like talking to a family member. As we began to talk about the procedure and what was required to get the retainers replaced, we began to talk about our kids and how they were doing, and catching up on what had been going on in our lives. When it came to my time, I told her that I was writing a book on the topic of failure. Initially she was in a bit of a rush to get back to the conference call that she walked out of so that she could speak with me, but as I mentioned the book, she let go of the door handle, displayed an inquisitive look and said, "Tell me more."

I began to explain how I had multiple failures in my life and had learned a lot during these failures. I shared a couple of my failures that actually became my successes. I mentioned to her that I want to revolutionize how people see, understand, embrace, and respond to failures, changing those experiences from a negative to a positive experience, through writing and motivational speaking. At this point in our conversation, she forced a smile and a little sigh and shared with me that it was breaking her heart for her to hear her five-year-old son beating himself up and calling himself a failure when he didn't successfully complete as he wanted to, or when he lost in certain phases of his video games. It was unsettling for me to see her this sad and to hear that a five-year-old was literally calling himself a failure. She is a good mom and very loving person. She said she had done everything to encourage him, but nothing was working. She asked me how would I go about changing his attitude. First, I said, "There are no magic bullets when it comes to the topic of failure." Then I said I would explain to him that when we don't always accomplish some of our goals, it doesn't mean we are failures. I suggested that she explain to him that even when he fails, it's not a *bad* thing, but an opportunity to learn from not achieving a goal. This would help him understand that winning should never be his only option, but rather, *learning* is something he should always be interested in.

I didn't tell my orthodontist anything she wasn't already aware of. The issue was that, as much as she loved her son, the topic of failure was uncomfortable to talk about. Especially in a world where every kid gets a trophy, even if they don't deserve it. By the end of our conversation her spirits were lifted, and she was laughing at what I assumed was my excitement as I shared with her my idea about failure.

By the way, after I had scheduled the appointment, my daughter ended up finding her retainers. Where were they? In her bed, under the covers. She was so tired from attending her high school prom that she forgot to take them out of her mouth in her bathroom.

In the end, there were great lessons learned about failure, how to teach others about failing, and how to handle not accomplishing goals, whether it be a teenager who lost her dental retainers momentarily, a dad who could have handled the situation with better understanding and patience, or a mom frustrated with trying to get her five-year-old to not consider himself a failure. In all of these situations, it is best to remain positive and not focus on the negative.

$$F+RR=S$$

Failure + Right Response = Success

Chapter Twenty-Eight

A FailureTastic Moment

"The future belongs to those who believe in the beauty of their dreams."
-Eleanor Roosevelt

When it comes to your personal failures, own them! No one gets to decide our failures for us. I was at an appointment with my physical therapist at our base military facility in Fort Lee, Virginia, which, in my opinion, is one of the best-equipped medical facilities (if not the best medical facility my family I have had the pleasure of being served by). From a clinician and customer service standpoint, on a scale of 1-10, I would easily give them 9.5. As this dedicated Army Captain and I were trading family stories and conversations, he and I got onto the topic of one of my favorite subjects: failure. I mentioned to him that I was writing a book and looking into becoming a motivational speaker and trainer on failure. He shared with me that he had experienced a lot of failure, and I shared very candidly with him that so had I. He asked if I would share an experience where I had failed. Sometimes our troops forget that even at the most senior levels within our military, lots of us fail. I shared with him how difficult it was for me to get into the Army initially, and how I was told repeatedly that I would never be an officer once I finally gained entry into the greatest fighting force on the planet.

He began to share a very personal story about how when he was a student in the Army's Baylor Medical Program, he had failed an exam. This program is a nationally-ranked physical therapy doctoral program which recruits and selects highly qualified individuals from the civilian sector to join the military, and who eventually can become officers in the U.S. Army or the U.S. Navy if they so choose. This program also selects applicants from within the active duty and reserve forces to transfer into its program from other Military Occupational Specialties. Following basic initial entry training into this program, these officers engage in thirty months of entry-level physical therapy training and, if successful, will receive the Doctor of Physical Therapy degree (DPT).

Upon commencement, these graduates are well-prepared to serve in two unique professions: as an active-duty officer, and as a military physical therapist. He began to share with me how arrogant he was during that time. He told himself that he already knew everything about the profession and how easy it was going to be for him to graduate from the program. He explained that, to his surprise, his first practical exercise was not as easy as he first thought. He received a letter grade of C. For some, that would have been not perfect, but it was good enough for him. For this motivated officer, he said that letter grade was, to him, a failure. At most educational institutions, a C is not failing, but for him it was.

That one episode of failure (as he considered it to be) did not stop him. In fact, the high-speed captain said that it was a great lesson in humility, and motivated him to go on from there to receive excellent grades for the rest of the course.

I can personally and professionally, with great confidence and after interacting with this Army officer for almost two years on a consistent basis, give him "a go at this station." captain H is one of the most committed and technically proficient Army officers I have ever had the honor of serving with. He made it clear to me that his failure was what gave him the determination to work harder and become the best physical therapist in the U.S. Army. This is what I call a great "FailureTastic" moment. FailureTastic is a term I use when I hear of someone who experienced a potentially career-ending or potentially insurmountable failure, but instead of giving up, giving in, or quitting, they dig in, keep pounding sand, and they turn that failed experience into a success.

F+RR=S

Failure + Right Response = Success

What was the high-speed Captain's response to his failure?

Chapter Twenty-Nine
<u>MY DAUGHTER'S FAILURE</u>

"Failure is not the problem®; It is the beginning of your success."
-George Milton

My daughter learned a very valuable lesson today. She wanted to join her high school track and field team. Mentally, she convinced herself that she was ready. Equipment-wise, she wasn't totally prepared, but she figured she could wing it. I decided that she needed the proper equipment and promptly took her to several shoe stores to find a pair of running shoes. After finding a pair, she assured me while in the store the shoes fit. I asked her repeatedly if they *truly* fit, and she reassured me that they did.

After a day or so of practices, she came home and told me that the shoes were too big. What? I wanted to know what happened between the time when she said they fit in the store to when she came home and said they no longer fit. "Know before you go" was the first lesson she learned.

The next day she had her time trials and field event tryouts. I arrived at the track as planned to pick her up. As she approached me, she began crying. I asked what was wrong, and she told me she didn't make the team. She put her backpack and workout clothes in the car. After doing so, I hugged her as she cried profusely. My heart hurt deeply for her. I tried to comfort her as we drove home. As tears were streaming down her face, I said that I was very proud of her for trying. Then we had a conversation as to whether or not she had prepared properly so she could compete well, thereby maximizing her opportunity to make the team. I asked her if she thought she had trained well enough to make the team, to which she admitted that she had not. I mentioned to her that she possessed the athletic ability, but had not taken the proper time and preparation that some of the other kids who made the team had. She accepted that. I reinforced to her that failing to make the team wasn't the problem. As she well knows, life is full of challenges and failures, and had she prepared properly, she could have made the team. I said to her that I thought what she *really* wanted to do was make the team so she could socialize, to which she smiled and began to laugh. Of all my children, she is the "social butterfly" of the family. Yes, making the team would have been a tremendous accomplishment for her, but the lesson in failure and her acceptance of her failure was a more purposeful and greater achievement.

Chapter Thirty
POTENTIAL FAILURE IS WORTH THE RISK

"Everybody's got something that they are good at, the hard part is finding it."
-Mark Cuban

I once heard Steve Harvey quote T. D. Jakes in saying,"I would hate to die, and never do the thing I was born to do. I think that would be the ultimate failure." Why not have mini failures along the way through life, getting you to the place you were destined to be, instead of being afraid of failing at all? Remember: *failure is not the problem*. Failure is a great way of figuring out your destiny, if only you can embrace it as a learning experience instead of allowing it to keep you from excelling at what you were born to be and do. I believe everyone was born to do something very specific. Maybe it's not just one simple thing, maybe it is. What's simple for you and me may very well be monumental for someone else. Either way, you need to figure out your purpose. Nothing in life is worthwhile unless you take risks. In taking risks, you're destined to fail.

While serving in the Army, I always wanted to jump out of airplanes. This required me going to Airborne School, or as it's fondly otherwise referred to, "jump school." Let's back up for a second. I knew that jump school would be fun and cool, but I also knew that being jump-qualified could potentially enhance my career. After all, that's what Army officers did. Being jump-qualified was almost like an unspoken rule. If you wanted to be an Officer, you needed jump wings. In order to get those coveted airborne wings, I knew I would have to jump out of an aircraft, which involved the highest of all risks: not merely failure, but death. During my training, I had two incidents which could have deterred me from completing my training and thus ended my dream of becoming jump qualified.

When you jump out of an aircraft, there are a number of procedures and checks and balances that need to be performed to ensure the chute will be properly deployed and will fill up with enough air to guarantee a safe ride to the ground. Once you exit the aircraft, you are taught to look up, checking the canopy and canopy straps to ensure there are no entanglements. As I tried to raise my head from the tucked position as we were instructed, I could not raise my neck or head to check my canopy or the straps. "Danger Will Robinson--Danger!" Failure! Or was it? Automatically and immediately, I performed the safety measures taught to me to get myself out of this potentially life-ending scenario. As I had learned in training, should this ever happen, simply begin slowly pumping your knees up and down as though you're riding a bicycle. Miraculously, it worked. Imagine that, the training actually worked. I stopped my rapid descent, regained my composure, and the ride down was fantastic.

The second event happened during another jump while making a landing on the ground. As described before, I exited the aircraft, and all went well. The problem this time was that I was enjoying the wonders of the sky above and the beauty of the earth below. This was a good ride, so much so that I forgot to perform a correct PLF, or what the Army Airborne School called a Parachute Landing Fall. Oops! Yeah, this is pretty important. A parachute landing fall (PLF) is a safety technique that is designed to allow a parachutist to land safely and without injury. The technique is performed by paratroopers and recreational parachutists alike. The technique is used to displace the energy of the body contacting the earth at high speeds. The parachutist ideally lands facing the direction of travel with feet and knees together. At the moment that first contact is made with the ground, the person goes from an upright position to absorbing the impact by allowing the body to buckle and go toward a horizontal position, while rotating toward the side (generally the direction with the dominant directional speed).

When executed properly, this technique is capable of allowing a parachutist to survive uninjured during landing speeds that would otherwise cause severe injury or even death. As I approached the ground, I was supposed to take my knees and pull them up together while looking straight ahead and not at the ground. I did neither. I can only describe the pain as similar to when we were kids and our parents told us to not ride our bikes without a seat (but we did it anyway), and as luck would have it, while we were pretending to be Evil

Kenevil making that big jump, you'd land on the bar (which, thank God for our butt bone, or who knows what would have happened, or where that protruding rod might have gone). Pain shot from my toes to the top of my head, and the scream I belted out was so loud that the folks working in the local shipyard thought it was lunchtime whistle! That's how intense the pain was.

Once again, failure. But it was worth the risk, because the end result was that I continued with my training, continued going up in the aircraft, continued jumping out of aircraft, and eventually graduating and earning those beautiful jump wings, having fun along the way. *Failure wasn't the problem*, it was my success. It motivated me even more and made me more determined to get it right and become successful at obtaining my jump wings. *Hooah!*

Chapter Thirty-One

STRUGGLE IS GOOD! I WANT TO FLY

"Kaizen"
-Japanese term meaning "change for the better."

Once, a little boy was playing outdoors and found a fascinating caterpillar. He carefully picked it up and took it home to show his mother. He asked his mother if he could keep it, and she said he could, if he would take good care of it. The little boy got a large jar from his mother and put plants in it for the caterpillar to eat and a stick for it to climb on. Every day, he watched the caterpillar and brought it new plants to eat. One day the caterpillar, climbed up the stick and started acting strangely. The boy worriedly called his mother who came and understood that the caterpillar was creating a cocoon. The mother explained to the boy how the caterpillar was going to go through a metamorphosis and become a butterfly.

The little boy was thrilled to hear about the changes his caterpillar would go through. He watched every day, waiting for the butterfly to emerge. One day it happened. A small hole appeared in the cocoon, and the butterfly started to struggle to come out. At first the boy was excited, but soon he became concerned. The butterfly was struggling so hard to get out! It looked like it couldn't break free. It looked so desperate! It looked like it was making no progress. The boy was so concerned that he decided to help. He ran to get scissors, and then walked back (because he had learned not to run with scissors). He snipped the cocoon to make the hole bigger and the butterfly quickly emerged!

As the butterfly came out, the boy was surprised. It had a swollen body and small, shriveled wings. He continued to watch the butterfly, expecting that, at any moment, the wings would dry out, enlarge and expand to support the swollen body. He thought that in time, the body would shrink, and the butterfly's wings would expand. But neither happened. The butterfly spent the rest of its life crawling around with a swollen body and shriveled wings; it never was able to fly.

As the boy tried to figure out what had gone wrong, his mother took him to talk to a scientist from a local college. He learned that the butterfly was *supposed* to struggle. In fact, the butterfly's struggle to push its way through the tiny opening of the cocoon pushes the fluid out of its body and into its wings. Without the struggle, the butterfly would never, ever fly. The boy's good intentions hurt the butterfly.[13]

---

[13] http://instructor.mstc.edu/instructor/swallerm/Struggle%20-%20Butterfly.htm

As you go through life, keep in mind that struggling is an important part of any growth experience. In fact, it is the struggle that causes you to develop your ability to fly. The Army has allowed me the opportunity to travel the world and participate in some amazing, rewarding events. It has also allowed me to be challenged in some interesting ways. I've been in extreme cold and extreme heat, and traveled to (and lived in) faraway lands that I could only ever dream about as a child. Yes, I've even been in very dangerous situations. In some of these experiences, I was out of my element and totally uncomfortable. What I learned throughout those experiences was that in order to reach my goals, I had to learn how to be resilient. In other words, I had to learn how to be comfortable in uncomfortable situations. Regarding failure, I had to learn how to be comfortable with failing. In the same way that my challenges in those faraway lands and environments gave me opportunities, so have my failures.

You've probably heard the mantra that failure is not an option. Of course failure is an option! In fact, it's more than just an option, it's guaranteed! Failure is a part of our daily lives. *Failure is not the problem*®. How we perceive it and respond to it and react to it is generally the problem, not failure! Failure is the beginning of your success! If you are afraid of failure, you're already failing. Moving beyond failure takes courage. Allowing failure to keep you from becoming all that you can be is--guess what--failure! Why do we try our entire lives to avoid failure when it's like breathing: necessary in order to live?

In order to move beyond failure, you must set goals. Why set goals? Because if you're serious about moving beyond failure, setting goals can help you stay focused. If you don't fail from time to time, it's a sure sign you've been playing it safe.

So, go fail. Go get it wrong, but in the process, learn and grow.

-George Milton, The Failure Coach

About the Author

George Milton is a recently retired career Army officer who traveled to and lived in roughly 40 different countries. An Army Officer Candidate School Hall of Famer. A guy who barely graduated from high school, yet went on to earn four degrees-two of which are master's level, one from the largest seminary in the world, Southwestern Baptist Theological Seminary, where he earned 17 hours toward a doctorate before leaving the program to become an Assistant University Professor in Military Science at Northwestern State University of Louisiana; and the other from the United States Army War College.

Although he has incredible accomplishments, which has taken him and his family to a lot of fun and exciting places, there have also been many disappointments.

It was because of his failure that he learned how to turn his disappointments into positive outcomes.

He currently lives in Virginia and is the Chief Executive Officer of Failure Is Not The Problem, LLC., a consulting and leadership training company, as well as a life coach and motivational speaker.

Made in the USA
Monee, IL
07 March 2020